CALLED! STEP BY STEP

JUNE HALL MCNEELY
with
JOYCE SWEENEY MARTIN

authorHOUSE®

AuthorHouse™
1663 Liberty Drive
Bloomington, IN 47403
www.authorhouse.com
Phone: 1 (800) 839-8640

Published by AuthorHouse   04/21/2015

ISBN: 978-1-5049-0746-0 (sc)
ISBN: 978-1-5049-0745-3 (e)

Print information available on the last page.

Any people depicted in stock imagery provided by Thinkstock are models,
and such images are being used for illustrative purposes only.
Certain stock imagery © Thinkstock.

This book is printed on acid-free paper.

CONTENTS

To Gerald – partner in life, partner in ministry –
and to
our daughters and their husbands:
Linda and Rusty,
Marsha and David

FOREWORD

I became acquainted with the legacy of June and Gerald McNeely in the early 1980s when I was a seminarian working for the *Western Recorder*, the newspaper for the Kentucky Baptist Convention, and became engaged to their youngest daughter, Marsha. As I was covering a Kentucky Baptist event, Chauncey Daley, who was editor of the Western Recorder, introduced me to a group of prominent Kentucky Baptist pastors by saying, "He's engaged to the McNeely girl." They beamed approvingly, giving me instant (though unjustified) celebrity.

When I met June and Gerald a few months later, I found they pretty much lived up to the legacy.

The McNeelys, of course, never intended to be legends. They simply intended to be faithful to take the next step in God's plan. Over the course of their lives, sometimes the step was a small one, taking a pastorate, learning and implementing lessons along the way. Other steps were bigger – even ocean's length – to tell the Gospel's story to people who had access only to state-sponsored religion.

While through the years I've heard most of the stories in this book, I've never heard them in context as June narrates them here. The episodes of persecution, disappointment, small and then larger victories are so much more vivid, moving, and inspiring when set against the backdrop of a dictatorial regime fixated on eradicating dissention. This book often moved me to goose bumps and even tears. Honestly, if I weren't already appointed, I think I'd become a missionary. I was truly sad when I got to the end, feeling that I had lost something.

This is an inspiring, vital, and instructive work. While many of us look at the enormity of the task and are overwhelmed by it, the McNeelys exemplify being faithful to do the next right thing, surmount the upcoming obstacle, and take the next step.

Gerald and June are the missionaries all newly minted missionaries think they will be on the night they are appointed.

David Smith
Missionary

PREFACE

❀

"A stroke? I've had a stroke? Then that must be why I can't move my right hand and arm, or my right leg."

I didn't know where I was or how I had gotten there. I did remember that I had fallen at home and I did remember hearing a key in the lock. I remember being lifted from an ambulance and thinking that several other patients were on gurneys behind me.

I stayed in the hospital for five days, but I have no memory of that. Then I was transferred to a rehab facility. I remember hearing someone say, "That one won't leave here alive." I remember thinking "that one" was the person on the gurney following mine. (Later, I was told that I was the "one" the nurse had been talking about and there was no gurney following mine.) My family rallied around me and provided loving support. I am especially gratefully for my brother, Keith, who regularly drove almost sixty miles to sit with me and feed me.

The rehab facility had excellent physical therapists. To them, I wasn't just a patient. I was a person with feelings. I will always think of those therapists with gratitude. They helped me regain the use of my right hand and my right side. (A previous stroke had left damage, so that was not my first experience with the humbling feeling of helplessness.)

My therapists encouraged me to write as a way of retraining my right hand. My family encouraged me to think of memories that I might want to share with them. They felt that would give me something concrete to focus on. And they were correct.

And so, four years ago, that is how this book began. Over these last four years, as I was writing I thought I was recording events and stories to be read only by my family about my growing-up years in Stanford, Kentucky; my college years; my years as a pastor's wife; and my thirty-three years with Gerald as a Southern Baptist missionary in Spain. And so, with that in mind, I wrote and wrote, eventually filling more than 120 pages with my handwritten remembrances.

Then something happened. My family began to tell me that my story needed a wider audience than just my family. They began to tell me that my story could help young men and women who are struggling with God's claim on their lives. They told me that how I had responded to God's call to international missions would inspire other believers to follow God wherever He leads.

My random memories first recorded as therapy became the basis for *CALLED! Step by Step*. My prayer is that God will use this book to bring glory to Him. To that end, I give it to Him and I leave how He will use it in His hands.

June Hall McNeely
Age 90
Louisville, Kentucky
April 2015

Trust in the Lord with all your heart
And lean not on your own understanding;
In all your ways acknowledge Him,
and He will direct your paths.
Proverbs 3: 5-6

ONE

❁

"hy did you go to Spain?" Over the last fifty-eight years, Gerald and I have been asked that question dozens of times and we've always given the same answer: "The decision was easy. God called us there." We've never doubted our call, our preparation, or serving the Lord so far away from family.

For many people, the concept of a call from God to spend one's life in another country and in an unfamiliar culture is baffling. But for those who have experienced that call, it is simply reassuring; it's not a call to hardship, rather it's a tender call to something that is a perfect fit. For Gerald and me, throughout our years in Spain – in times of frustration and discouragement as well as in times when we saw ministry dreams fulfilled – we could always return to the certainty that we were exactly where God wanted us, doing exactly what He wanted us to do. Many times over the years we thanked God for His call to us to serve Him in Spain.

❁

I REMEMBER THE exact spot where I was sitting when I first felt that call to be a missionary. I was about twelve years old and was attending a missions meeting for girls (Girls Auxiliary) in our leader's home in Stanford, Kentucky. As I sat on a hassock near the fireplace and our leader prayed, I felt a strong sense of "that's for me" and "this is right". Looking back, I don't think I realized it was a call; rather, I thought of it as a special "something".

1

At my church, Stanford Baptist, in my childhood, loving members had helped me to learn that God loves us so much that He sent Jesus to die for us and show us how we can serve Him. They had taught me that as Christians we are to show love to and share love with others. They had provided many opportunities to study about missions and missionaries in our mission organizations, which I loved. Indeed, they had prepared the way for God to speak to a twelve-year-old girl such as myself. In many ways, members of Stanford Baptist were like extended family. They were strong examples of how to live as Christians.

My mother, Nancy Ratliff Hall, was my most important example and mentor. She was a beautiful Christian who wanted each one of her five children to know Christ and serve Him. Mother was a wise woman who loved her children dearly, and we were secure in her love. To us, she was our angel whom we adored. She not only set an example for us but also often sacrificed so we could have things we needed or wanted. She was a humble woman who was always ready to help others. I grew up with the belief that life is about serving God.

Indeed, Mother had a tender spot for people in need. Because I was born in 1924 and grew up in the middle of the Great Depression, I often saw needy people in our town. Men often came to our front porch asking for food and Mother never refused them. She would tell them to wait while she prepared something for them. She would then serve them on the porch. Mother always served them hearty meals and never let anyone go away hungry. Because Mother grew a large vegetable garden and canned/ preserved everything she could, our family always had food to eat and share. We also had our own chickens – which provided eggs and meat – and Daddy raised and butchered two hogs each year. And like most people in our community, we ate lots of pinto beans and cornbread.

One day we saw a strange marking on our front gate. We soon found out it was a mark to tell men – tramps, as they were called – who had lost their jobs during the Depression that they could always find food at our home.

My father, John M. Hall, had a heart as tender as Mother's where hungry people were concerned. One day he told Mother about an elderly black man who lived in a shack near the railroad tracks and suggested that Mother prepare some food he could take to him. She not only prepared food for the man that day but also many times after that. Later Daddy asked if Mother had an extra blanket he could take to the man. Mother gave him a double blanket, which was twice as long as a regular blanket and would have made a very warm covering. (Daddy didn't attend church with us and didn't become a Christian until later in his life, but we children knew he loved us and had high standards for all of us. Most often, he didn't tell us what to do or not to do but he would tell Mother to tell us. Plus, she was the parent who meted out punishment.)

Looking back, I think Daddy had developed a tender heart early in his life. When his mother was dying of breast cancer at about age forty, she had asked him – as the oldest of eight children – to take care of his father and his siblings. Even though he was only sixteen years old, Daddy promised her that he would. Over the next years, he kept his promise, often in remarkable and strange ways. Daddy followed his father to several places around Pikeville, Kentucky, to live and work that he never would have considered if not for the promise he'd made to his mother. Later, he tried to teach his father how to drive but soon gave up and hired a driver for him. At the time, his father owned a hotel in Pikeville and relied totally on his eldest son to help him. He also bought a restaurant near the hotel and depended on Daddy to run it. Daddy was a good cook – and true to his nature – never complained.

❊

IT WAS MY MOTHER'S father, my Grandfather Henry Ratliff, who introduced me to the Bible. When he and Grandmother Mary Hughes Ratliff made their annual visit from their home in Eastern Kentucky, I dearly loved sitting on his lap while he read the Bible to me. I'm sure I didn't understand what he was reading, but I did understand that what he was doing was important to him and, thus, it should be important to me. His love for Scripture helped me to love the Bible, too. I can still hear him saying, "Now, little daughter, this means...." Plus, I knew he loved me.

Many years later, Grandpa went blind. One day I saw Grandmother Ratliff standing outside their bedroom door watching him as he sat by the window, seemingly talking aloud to no one. "Oh, Grandmother, he's talking," I said. "He must want something." "No, Honey," she replied, "He's just 'reading' his Bible." You see, he'd read his Bible so often that in his blindness he could still "read" it. That put me to shame as I wondered how I could have failed to memorize Scripture as my grandfather had done. (Interestingly, my sister Edna had a similar experience with watching him "read" his Bible and hearing Grandmother's response.)

❧

LOOKING BACK, what I would later understand as the call to be a missionary when I was twelve set the course of my life. At the time I didn't tell anyone, much less know what its import would be. I thought of it as something very private to be kept in my heart. It never even occurred to me share it with anyone. When I was fourteen, I attended a youth missions (Girls Auxiliary) camp and made a public profession of faith in Jesus as my Savior and Lord. At that camp, I met a real live missionary who was serving in Japan. I was deeply impressed as she told of her life in Japan and talked about the need for the Gospel there. Still, I told no one about the nudging toward missions that I was experiencing.

It wasn't until about sixteen years after that moment in Stanford that God confirmed my call to missions. I no longer merely had a sense that God had something special for me to do with my life; I had a definite call to foreign/international missions. Between my twelfth year and my twenty-eighth year, God prepared me for what only He knew lay ahead.

For it is by grace that you have been saved though faith –
And this is not from yourself.
It is the gift of God – not by works
so no one can boast. For we are God's workmanship,
created in Christ Jesus to do good works.
Ephesians 2: 8-9

TWO

❀

Family, church, and school were the three intertwining threads around which life in the Hall family revolved. And in each of those realms, God gave me exceptional mentors – people who helped me see and begin to realize my possibilities.

First and foremost among those mentors was my mother. As I wrote in chapter one, she was an example of Christian love and sacrifice. Many times she reminded me that doctors had told her that she would never have children, but after she and Daddy had been married five years, I was born on Dec. 20, 1924. Mother wanted to name me Beverly after the heroine in a book she'd been reading, but Daddy didn't like that name and insisted on a shorter name to go with Beverly. Since his name is John, I became June. I didn't know my first name is Beverly until I started first grade.

I wasn't to be an only child, for two years later along came Ernestine, followed by Edna one year later, and then Mary Catherine three years after her. Then, after four girls, three years later came a boy – our baby brother, Keith. I was ten years old when Keith was born.

Mother enjoyed listening to Christian programs on the radio and also enjoyed listening to opera on Saturday afternoons. In fact, she usually saved her ironing to do then; she didn't like to waste time even if it was to listen to something she enjoyed. She was a multi-tasker long before the word was in vogue. When she wasn't listening to the radio, she often sang the hymn "In the Garden" as she worked.

Mother loved to read and she encouraged us children to read, too. She also liked to tell us how much she'd enjoyed the spelling bees when she was growing up in rural Pike County, Kentucky, in the heart of Appalachia. Daddy grew up in the same community, and they both attended the same two-room school that housed grades one through eight. Because Daddy was two years older than Mother and was an excellent speller, he thought he was entitled to win all the spelling contests. Mother, however, wasn't going to let that tall, handsome boy win all of them, and so she – a short, diminutive girl – made sure she won as many as he did. You can imagine how proud they both were when I – their eldest child – began spelling out words and reading advertisements.

Both Mother and Daddy always took an active interest in all their children's education. When I started first grade, they were almost as excited as I was. Daddy had lots of advice for me, as his oldest child. He showed me how to hold my hands "just so" on my desk. He told me that when my teacher called my name as she took the roll each day, I was to answer, "Present," and he explained what that meant. Imagine how shocked I was when some of my classmates answered roll call with "Here" and when some sat with their feet in the aisle instead of putting them under their desks. I was sure they would be punished, but they weren't.

When I was old enough to have a spelling book – in second grade, I think – Daddy considered it his duty to read my spelling words to me. Sometimes he would look in the back of my book and ask me to spell harder words than the ones I'd been assigned. When I would spell one of those harder words correctly, he would look over at Mother and grin as if to say, "See, she takes after me." I don't think they ever wanted to forget their spelling bee rivalry in their school days in Pike County.

I must confess that I made only one spelling mistake in twelve years of school – and to this day I remember exactly what it was. The word was *kitchen*, which I spelled correctly. However, I momentarily forgot how to make a lower case *k*, so the word was marked as incorrect. Believe me, it took a long time to live that down.

During my elementary years, I was always so proud that Mother attended our Parent-Teacher Association (PTA) meetings at Stanford Elementary. She may not have been the most fashionable mother there, but I always thought she was the prettiest.

My first grade teacher, Miss Annie McKinney, was one of my first non-family mentors. She was a strict grammarian. Even today in 2015, when someone makes a grammatical error or misspells a word I automatically think – and sometimes say aloud – "I can tell you didn't have Miss Annie McKinney for your first grade teacher."

My dad's brother, Uncle Willie Hall, was also an important mentor. A respected educator, he taught history at Stanford High School. It was he who gave me my first grown-up book, *Eight Cousins* by Louisa Mae Alcott. It was the first book that was really mine; I don't have any idea how many times I read it, but it was a lot. Looking back, I have no doubt that it had much to do with my life-long love of books. Uncle Willie loved history and had an amazing memory for both history and the Bible. He also was very exacting in his speech and writing. One Sunday when I was eating dinner with his family, I was shocked when one of his daughters told him he'd made a grammatical error in his prayer in the church service that morning. I was deeply offended because I believed my Uncle Willie didn't make mistakes.

❀

MY ELEMENTARY DAYS came to a close and I moved on to attend Stanford High School. In addition to family, other people soon were added to my growing list of mentors. (Of course, Uncle Willie continued his interest in my education. He even came to Stanford High my freshman year to make sure I'd enrolled in the classes he thought were best suited to me.)

I soon learned that for me the most important thing in the entire school was the library, over which Miss Marian Grimes ruled. I marveled that she got to read all those wonderful books.

Sometimes I stayed after school to help her. Thankfully, she quickly saw how much I liked to read and encouraged me by suggesting books she thought I'd enjoy. She especially noticed how much I liked biographies and often showed me new ones the library had just received.

And then one day Miss Grimes suggested I enter a state-wide contest and write on the theme, "What the Library Means to Me." That was easy. When she read my theme, she didn't correct any part of it. I thought that was the end of the story and even forgot about writing the essay – until Miss Grimes received a phone call telling her that I had won the state contest. The prize was a book. She was as excited as I was – if that was possible. I even made the headlines in the next issue of the school paper.

Jo Platt, a typing and shorthand teacher at Stanford High who was also a member of Stanford Baptist, became another of my mentors. She first showed her confidence in me by giving me the responsibility of caring for the plants on the window ledge in her classroom. When I stayed after school to take care of the plants, she and I talked about our church and its teachings. We talked about Jesus and how He gave His life for us. Then she asked me to be a teacher's helper in her Sunday school (Bible study) class of eight-year olds. That was a wonderful experience, which I took very seriously. I wanted to be able to answer any and all the questions those children asked. I learned much from Miss Platt, including the importance of Bible study for even eight-year-olds.

I also learned that the responsibility of Sunday school teachers often extends beyond the classroom. Sometimes Miss Platt invited me to accompany her as she visited in the homes of her pupils, especially those whose parents didn't attend church. After our visits, she would take me to her home for lunch, which usually was a grilled cheese sandwich. She said that was the only thing she knew how to cook.

Another member of Stanford Baptist became a mentor as well. Mr. W.H.W. Reynolds was the leader of our Baptist Youth group of which I was president. He was highly respected both as a leader in the church and as an attorney. One summer he asked if I would work for him, typing papers that he needed. I agreed. Much of the typing concerned Stanford Baptist Church. I typed business meeting minutes and lists of committee members, among other things. And I greatly enjoyed doing research on other non-church matters at the county courthouse.

At some point during the summer Mr. Reynolds asked me if I thought I'd like to be an attorney, and we discussed that possibility. While I did enjoy working for him, I didn't find becoming an attorney appealing, especially after I had to type a letter to a family with a long- unpaid grocery bill and with little money to pay the debt.

As a result of working with Mr. Reynolds, I was given the responsibility of setting up and managing the files for the Lincoln County rationing board. World War II had begun when I was fifteen and a sophomore in high school. Rationing boards had quickly been set up across the country to help ensure that all needed food and supplies were going to the Allies in Europe. Every family was issued rationing coupons to use to purchase coffee, sugar, meat, cheese, butter, canned goods, gasoline, clothing, shoes, and other items. Without a coupon, no one could buy any of those things. The coupons had to be picked up at a rationing board site. My task was to keep the records of those pick-ups.

The soldiers away in the war had long been a part of our lives. I'd helped Mother fold bandages for wounded soldiers at our local Red Cross chapter, and in high school I had the responsibility of carrying a box of saving stamps from classroom to classroom for students to purchase. The stamps cost very little and could be traded for savings bonds.

❈

ONE SUMMER DURING my high school years, youth from four evangelical churches in Stanford decided to join forces. When we met for the first time, the youth surprised me by electing me president. I was honored. That summer we held regular meetings and activities in the four churches. We also decided that beyond just meeting for fellowship and games, we should find a need in our town and try to meet it.

A few months before, Mother's missionary group at Stanford Baptist had cleaned the home of a blind man and his handicapped daughter, and Mother had invited me to help them. I thought our newly-formed youth group could do something to help the man and his daughter, especially since he spent most of his time sitting alone in his front porch swing. I suggested that our group take turns just sitting and talking with him or perhaps reading to him. He always looked so lonely. My suggestion was accepted with enthusiasm, and all the youth participated. Looking back, I already was learning that I had a real interest in ministry.

❈

ALL TOO QUICKLY my high school years came to an end and it was time for college. While I had enjoyed my school days, I had no idea what adventures lay ahead.

Do nothing out of selfish ambition or vain conceit,
but in humility consider others better than yourself.
Philippians 2:3

THREE

❀

In 1943, I graduated from Stanford High School and set my sights toward college. During my senior year, Mother and I had studied college information and had talked with representatives from several colleges who came to recruit at Stanford High. Both Mother and I had been impressed with what we'd learned about Virginia Intermont, a girls' school in Bristol, Virginia. We knew it was expensive but felt it would be affordable if I could work. When I asked about the possibility of working in the library, the school's representative said that the only requirement would be that I take one course in Library Science, preferably "classification of books" – just what I wanted. I applied to Virginia Intermont (VI) and at the same time applied to work in the library. I was accepted for both.

When it came time for me to leave for college, I took the train from Stanford to Bristol, which was 200 miles away. It was the first long trip I made by myself. Even though it was a direct route and I wouldn't have to change trains, Daddy was worried about a particular town that the train would pass through because it had a bad reputation. He knew that large numbers of soldiers boarded the train there. When the train arrived at that station, I watched as soldiers boarded the already-crowded train. They were tired and some of them slept on the floor. Others sat on their luggage and rested their heads on the arms of seats and slept. I didn't have to get off the train there, so I had no problems.

When I arrived in Bristol, someone from the college met me and when I arrived at my room, my trunk was already there. For the first time in my life, I was on my own without my family. I was ready for a new adventure.

❁

AT VIRGINIA INTERMONT, I found new adventures at every turn. I was surrounded by beautiful girls who were much more sophisticated than I, a shy girl from a small town in Kentucky. At VI, we were expected to be ladies. We could leave campus on Mondays if we had special permission. We couldn't eat anything on the street – not even popcorn or ice cream. We had to wear hose, hats, and gloves when we went shopping. If we didn't have hose, we pretended. In my mind's eye even in 2015, I can see a girl standing on a chair as another girl with eyebrow pencil in hand is drawing a line down the back of her leg – at the time, hose were silk and always had a seam down the center of the back of the leg. Drawing the line made the girl look like she was actually wearing hose. Actually, looking back, those norms weren't that far from my mother's requirements for lady-like behavior in Stanford.

Many of the VI girls were from wealthy families in the eastern United States. They were beautiful and sophisticated. I knew about at least two upperclassmen who brought their horses to school and spent as much time polishing their saddles as they spent in class – the Boots and Saddle Club was the largest club on campus. They were not snobbish at all, however, and I did make many friends, mostly through the school's Baptist Student Union (BSU).

I developed a friendship with my first bi-lingual friend. Rosamund was the daughter of an American embassy official in El Salvador. She'd grown up there and had a Spanish accent that I thought was beautiful. That was the first time I'd ever heard a Spanish accent. Little did I know how natural those accents would sound to me in years yet to come. Rosamund and I became good friends. That Thanksgiving a couple from the church we both attended invited Rosamund and me to have Thanksgiving dinner with them. Since neither of us could be with our families, spending time together with that family kept us from feeling too homesick.

My mother helped me develop another friendship. The day I told her that the mother of a girl I knew in BSU had just died, Mother just happened to be preparing a package to send me, so she prepared one for the girl, too. She also included a short note with the package. When that became known at VI, several girls told me what an amazing mother I had. I already knew that.

I'd always been an avid reader, so in many ways life at Virginia Intermont was a confirmation of lifestyles and opportunities that had only existed for me in books. The girls from privileged and affluent backgrounds were no doubt familiar with all that the Intermont community had to offer, but for me those things were new.

For the first time in my life, I got to attend concerts, plays, and other special cultural events regularly. Since Bristol was home to two girls' junior colleges, the city offered many such events. For those events, we VI girls would don our long dresses and eagerly line up for the buses to take us to the venues. My favorite concert artist was the violinist Yehudi Menuhin. I'd always loved violin music but hadn't been able to study violin because there was no violin teacher in Stanford. (Granted, paying for lessons would have been a challenge for my parents even though they had managed to provide my sister Mary Catherine with piano lessons and my sister Ernestine with art lessons.)

At Intermont, for the first time in my life fiction turned into reality as girls who came from all across the country shared the stories of their lives, which were very different from mine. Even the more cosmopolitan and worldly-wise girls were friendly and respectful.

❁

AT INTERMONT, I became keenly aware of the effects World War II was having both in the U.S. and around the world. In Stanford, my work with the Lincoln County rationing board had been a constant reminder of the physical needs of the soldiers fighting in the war. But when several seniors at Stanford High had been drafted before they could graduate, the war had hit even closer to home.

At VI, I followed the war with an even greater urgency. In one of my courses, we were required to subscribe to the *New York Times* to better follow the war news. The professor posted a map of Europe in the entrance to the dining room and assigned each of us a day to follow the war in the *Times* and move thumbtacks to the places where fighting was occurring.

CALLED! STEP BY STEP

Also, several of the VI girls had boyfriends serving in the military and posted pictures of those young men in their rooms. Some of those young soldiers' pictures were even included in the school's yearbook.

We also tried to follow the path of the Jewish refugees whom Hitler was sending to concentration camps. That was hard for the Jewish girls in my class even if they had no friends or relatives among those involved. Again, even as the world was opening up around me, I still could only imagine what life would be like in places that I'd only read about.

My classes at VI were challenging. I especially enjoyed drama, though I never had a major role in a play. I also enjoyed journalism. I found my work in the library and a course in book classification especially enjoyable and satisfying. Even at that stage, however, I wasn't thinking of becoming a librarian. I wanted to be a teacher like my Uncle Willie.

❀

LOOKING BACK, I can see how God used my time at Virginia Intermont as yet another piece in the plan He had for my life. At VI, I met and interacted with girls from several states and even other countries. I sat in class with girls from very different social strata than mine. I talked with girls who practiced different religions than mine and with some who had no religion at all. I found I could adapt to these differences and still continue to live my Christian life. What preparation for my life's work in Spain!

Even though I still hadn't told anyone, I knew that God wanted me to do something special for Him. I soon learned that I didn't need to wait for Him to send me overseas: He had something special for me to do on the Intermont campus.

One day, one of the most sophisticated and most popular students asked a favor of me. She'd been assigned to introduce the speaker in Chapel and to lead a prayer in the service. She told me she didn't know how to pray and asked me to please write out a prayer that she could read at the service. I was surprised, to say the least. I'd never written a prayer in my life. In my Baptist tradition, we offered spontaneous prayers, not written prayers. But I did as she asked. Soon other girls began to make a similar request and I became known as "the freshman who prays". That opened the opportunity for me to talk to them about Jesus and to tell them how they could pray in their own words without having to ask someone to write a prayer for them.

❀

ATTENDING VIRGINIA Intermont proved to be too expensive for my parents, so I transferred to Georgetown College in Kentucky for my sophomore year. VI was also so far away from home that I'd only been able to come home at Christmas and at the end of the spring semester. On the other hand, Georgetown was sixty miles from Stanford – not 200 as was VI – and was near enough for me to come home on weekends.

Like VI, Georgetown was also a Baptist school, but unlike VI, it was co-ed. When I arrived on campus, many of the male students had served in the military and had returned home from the war to attend college. Little did I know just how much one of those men would impact my life.

Georgetown was a great fit for me. At the beginning of the summer term in 1945, I was sitting on the front porch of a girls' dorm helping a young man – who was my boyfriend at the time – with his French lesson when I saw some girls racing toward a car that had stopped at the nearby administration building.

Later those girls told me the rest of the story. It seems that a young man in a navy midshipman's uniform had just gotten out of his car, which led the girls to run to check him out. (My friend had asked if I wanted to go with them, but because I'd promised to help with his homework, I told him I wanted to finish that. "Besides," I said, "with all of those girls around him, he wouldn't notice me.") How wrong I was, even though it took a while for me to know that.

I learned the young man was wearing his uniform that day because he hadn't had time to buy civilian clothes; his uniform from the Naval Academy was all the clothes he had. Those girls had been most impressed.

The new student was Gerald McNeely – better known as Jerry. The next day I learned that he had enrolled in the same advanced English literature class as I. While I still hadn't met him, I had seen him and now we were sitting in adjoining seats in Dr. Coleman Arnold's class. (An aside: Many years later when our older daughter, Linda, was a student

17

at Georgetown, Dr. Arnold told her she should appreciate him because he had gotten her parents together. While that wasn't exactly true, it was true that Gerald and I had sat near the front of the classroom.) Over the course of the semester, I had no idea Gerald had noticed me even though I sometimes made excuses for him when he came late to class on Mondays. I knew he was a ministerial student studying to be a pastor and that he often preached on Sundays in churches some distance away. That meant he often arrived back on campus late on Sunday night and overslept the next morning.

That summer the college Baptist Student Union (BSU) of which I was a member volunteered to conduct Vacation Bible School (VBS) for an African-American church near the college. At first I didn't plan to help but because I was on the BSU missions committee, I decided I should. On the first morning, more helpers came than were expected, so I wasn't needed to teach. Instead, I was given the task of keeping a little girl from crying. She was too young to be in VBS, but there she was – and she became my responsibility. At least each time I picked her up, she stopped crying. But then if someone approached us, she would put her little arms tightly around my neck and begin to scream. She did the same thing if I tried to sit down. So I spent the entire morning carrying her around.

Jerry McNeely also was one of those "not needed" students that day. He'd come because he'd been elected vice president of the BSU – even though he was new on campus – and knew he, too, needed to come. Strangely, Gerald didn't even notice me that day. That still baffles me! How could he not notice a young woman with a screaming child in her arms?

By the end of the week, however, he had noticed me. By then, we were even walking back to campus together. To this day in 2015, we have a picture to prove it. (My daughter Linda says she has to wonder why we kept coming back all week when neither of us was needed. A mystery? Maybe. Maybe not.)

❇

OVER THE NEXT TWO YEARS, I continued to date several other boys. Gerald, however, seemed to me to be the only one really dedicated to Christian service, which was very important to me. As we began to get to know each other, I learned that while he'd grown up in the city of Louisville, Kentucky, and I in rural Lincoln County, we did have many things in common in addition to our Christian commitment. He, too, had been reared in a God-fearing family. In fact, his mother, Estelle Lawrence McNeely, had enrolled him in the cradle roll department of Walnut Street Baptist Church in Louisville shortly after his birth on Dec. 14, 1924, and she had kept his cradle roll certificate to prove it. (Gerald still has that certificate in 2015.) Later, his family had moved to south Louisville and joined Okolona Baptist Church. One pastor at Okolona Baptist, Dr. Howard Lee, had influenced Gerald greatly. Dr. Lee had taken a special interest in the youth in the church and had shown great confidence in them. One day during Vacation Bible School, he had given Gerald the keys to his car and asked him to run an errand for him – even though Gerald had only recently got his driver's license. That had impressed Gerald. Through the years, he would always remember how Dr. Lee preached about overcoming fear of an unknown future and trusting the Lord for guidance. How important that lesson would be when we set sail for Spain!

After graduating from Okolona High School in 1943, Gerald had enrolled in the University of Louisville but just before the first semester ended, he'd been drafted into the U.S. Army Air Corps to serve in World War II. He'd applied for pilot's training, but that didn't work out because at the time the Army had more pressing needs than pilots. Instead, Gerald had been assigned to attend Officers Training School in upstate New York. Later he'd been transferred to the Infantry. When it seemed that he wasn't going to be sent overseas, he and a group of friends had volunteered for the Army Paratroopers, expecting to be assigned to serve in Europe. After completing paratrooper training – including five jumps – he and his friends thought that at last they would be heading to active participation in the war.

Before that could happen, however, Gerald had learned that he was qualified to be appointed either to West Point Military Academy in New York or to the Naval Academy in Annapolis, Maryland. He had chosen the Naval Academy, had been discharged from the Army, and had enlisted in the Navy. He had been transferred to a Navy ship until time to enroll in the Academy. At the Academy, instruction for naval officers had emphasized math and science. Plus, he had studied German, which in future years would serve his family well.

Gerald's military career had been secure; his future, bright. But God had something else in mind: After one year at the Academy and two years in the military, God had called Gerald to Christian ministry. The natural thing would have been to become a military chaplain, especially since the Navy would have paid all Gerald's seminary expenses. He, however, had known that wasn't what God wanted for him: God was calling him to be a pastor. During his time at the Academy, he'd been greatly moved by the life and example of his pastor at the Baptist church he attended in Annapolis. He'd been especially impressed when the pastor had found a drunken man in the gutter in a street near the church, had taken the man home with him, sobered him up, and led him to faith in Christ as his personal Savior and Lord. And then, several days later, the pastor had bought the man a bus ticket, taken him to the station, and sent him home to a distant city where his wife was waiting for him. Gerald had never known anyone with such sacrificial interest in people. He thought the pastor personified Jesus. He knew that God was calling him to be a pastor in the full sense of the word: He wouldn't just preach, but he would also be a shepherd to his people.

And so, armed with his call from God to be a pastor, Gerald had resigned from the Navy and returned to Kentucky to enroll in Georgetown College. As for the other men in the group in his paratrooper training, they did make it to the war in Europe. Sadly, of the fourteen only one survived.

❀

AS FOR ME, after completing two years at Georgetown College, in the spring of 1947 I headed to Pittsburgh to the Western Pennsylvania School for the Deaf to fulfil a promise to a family friend to serve as a substitute teacher for one semester for someone who was having surgery. Since I was still seeking God's will for my life when this offer was made, I thought I would learn sign language while I was there. I thought that teaching the deaf might be one way God wanted to use me and I wanted to be prepared. Looking back, I realize that I was running ahead of God.

While I was in Pittsburgh, Gerald called me often and even came to visit me. Actually he came on a special mission: He asked me to marry him, and I said "Yes." We were married on Dec. 20, 1947, in the living room of my parents' home in Stanford. We chose to be married there in order for my sister Edna, who was in bed with rheumatic fever, to be able to watch the wedding through the open doorway of her bedroom. I thought my life course was set: I was to be a pastor's wife with a special interest in promoting missions.

The Lord watches the way of the righteous,
but the way of the wicked will perish.
Psalm 1:6

FOUR

✿

My first venture into the role of pastor's wife came at Ewing Baptist Church in the tiny town of Ewing in Fleming County in northern Kentucky. Over the next ten years, Gerald and I served three Kentucky churches.

Before we had married, Gerald had already been serving as interim pastor at Ewing Baptist while completing his senior year at Georgetown College. When he'd become interim pastor, the church had been a half-time church. That is, the church had shared a pastor with another Baptist church in the area and each church had held worship services every other Sunday. But soon after Gerald became pastor, he talked the people into becoming a full-time, services-every-Sunday church and even offered to accept a smaller pastoral salary if they would agree. They agreed to becoming a full-time church and giving Gerald what amounted to a half-time salary.

We'd been at Ewing just a few weeks when a woman in the church told Gerald she was sorry he'd married just before coming to the church. She said that the only reason she had voted for him to be the pastor was because he wasn't married. She further stated her reason: A wife would look for all of the dust in a house, but a man wouldn't notice. Thinking about that today makes me smile.

That spring semester, every Sunday we drove the fifty miles from Georgetown until Gerald graduated in the spring of 1948. After graduation we moved to Eastwood – about twenty miles east of Louisville – so that Gerald could begin working toward a master's degree at The Southern

Baptist Theological Seminary in Louisville that fall and I could begin teaching first grade at Simpsonville Elementary School in nearby Shelby County. (At the time, there was a shortage of teachers in Kentucky and one could teach without having completed four years of college. I had completed three.)

We moved into a small house next to Gerald's parents' home in Eastwood. They were very good to us, letting us live there rent-free and paying our utilities as well. I've always said I must have had the world's best parents-in-law. In fact, I've often said that I didn't have parents-in-law but instead had two sets of parents.

Gerald's mother seemed always to think of us as family, and I loved her for that. One day as I was in my classroom at Simpsonville Elementary, she came by for a visit. When she met one of my fellow teachers, she introduced herself as "June and Jerry's mother." I loved that.

Gerald's father, Clifton Coleman McNeely, was good to me, too. Because I was so tiny – about ninety pounds and five feet tall to be exact – and all Gerald's family members were of a larger build, it was sometimes difficult for him to treat me as an adult. A few days after Gerald and I married, we were with him and my mother-in-law in their car when he stopped at a railroad crossing. Before he thought, he said, "Junie girl, see the choo-choo train?" Gerald's mom was embarrassed but his dad simply said, "Well, she's the smallest one, isn't she?" Later that day as Gerald and I were leaving to return to Georgetown, I started to kiss him on his bald head. He laughed about that. My sweet mother-in-law said, "He won't wash that spot until the next time you're home."

❋

DURING THE TWO YEARS Gerald was pastor at Ewing Baptist we spent a lot of time on the road. Each week during the school year we drove to Ewing early on Sunday morning and returned to Eastwood late on Sunday night. Then during the summer months we lived on the field – that is, we lived in the church community – in Ewing.

Our first summer, we lived with Mrs. Sibley in two rooms of her small house. We cooked and ate on our half of her screened-in back porch. We had electricity but no running water and no indoor plumbing. We didn't have a refrigerator, so keeping milk was a problem. That was solved when I finally learned to drink coffee – an important social skill in the community – and found that I had to have milk in it in order to enjoy it. When Gerald explained the problem to Mrs. Sibley, she offered to let us keep milk in her icebox on her side of the porch. We found her to be a kind, sweet person, even if she did have her moments.

One day Mrs. Sibley was sitting on her front porch, talking with a neighbor. Gerald and I were inside but could hear the conversation clearly. Mrs. Sibley was telling her about a young bride who couldn't even cook green beans without burning them. All of a sudden a burning smell wafted out from the kitchen. Immediately, Mrs. Sibley jumped up and said, "My beans. They're burning." And they were.

I also remember her saying so many times, "I've buried two husbands and don't want another." I don't think she ever married again.

In Ewing, we learned that we could live simply. Many years later in Spain when our electricity would regularly go off, Gerald and I would remember our time in Ewing and simply be thankful when the electricity came back on. When we had to buy our drinking water in *garafas* (big glass water jugs), we knew we would be okay. Living in Ewing had taught us to be content, no matter the circumstances.

❀

GERALD AND I had a lot of firsts at Ewing Baptist. We led our first Vacation Bible School together. Over the years, I've sometimes said that Gerald married me because I had lots of experience in VBS. After all, it was in that VBS in Georgetown that we'd first really noticed each other.

That year when it came time for VBS, we were ready. My sister Mary Catherine came from Louisville to stay with us and play the piano for VBS. Our people were impressed because she knew by memory all the songs we sang as well as the stand-up and sit-down chords that were such an expected part of the VBS opening exercises/worship service in those days.

Because we had such limited living space as well as very little furniture, Mary Catherine slept on a cot in our living room. That was fine, except for the night the cot collapsed. Of course, that was the signal for Gerald to pull out his camera.

Gerald drove the church bus to transport the children to VBS each day. One sweet little girl named Linda impressed both of us greatly. She was always so well dressed, so neat and clean, and so well-behaved. We both fell in love with her. Later we visited her parents, but they never came to church while we were at Ewing. That year Gerald also planned special handwork for the boys. They worked with leather, making belts, and other things.

Another first was planning and directing Christmas programs together. One year, as part of the program the youngest children sang "Jesus Loves Me." The children sang beautifully. After they'd finished, they were to step back so another group could do their part. All the children except for one beautiful little girl stepped back. Even when all the others backed away, she stood alone, continuing to sing the chorus, "Yes, Jesus loves me. The Bible tells me so." Some people in the audience laughed, which made her nervous, but still she continued to sing. I knew it was time to do something without embarrassing the child or her parents and so I very slowly motioned to her to rejoin the other children and gently pulled her back as she continued to sing more softly and ever more softly. Her singing was beautiful and easily could have been planned as a part of the program. Little did I know that years later in Spain, I would have the privilege of writing and directing many church dramas.

For the first time, Gerald and I also experienced the kindness of a church family toward their pastor – whom they called "the little preacher" – and his family. Mrs. Lucy Grannis was especially kind to us. She often invited us to eat with her and her lovely daughter, Molly. The money for her beautiful and delicious meals came from her only income provided by her son who lived in Cincinnati. On one occasion when she'd just received a larger check than usual, she insisted on sharing it with us. Of course, we refused. Somehow she managed to slip it into Gerald's pocket. When we found it, we knew we had to figure out the best way to spend such a special gift even though we were on a tight budget ourselves.

On the way back to Eastwood that day, we decided to stop in Shelbyville to visit John and Alta Hatcher, good friends from our Georgetown days, who were starting a new church there and were living on an income even smaller than ours. When we got there, they told us they had been sitting in their trailer wondering what they could have for supper – they had no food. We immediately knew what we needed to do with Mrs. Grannis' gift. It couldn't have gone to two finer people. In later years, the Hatchers served as Southern Baptist missionaries in Brazil.

At Ewing we also learned to appreciate and love people in ways we had never loved before. We learned to accept people as they were and not try to change them, except to lead them to draw closer to Christ and to follow Him. In years yet to come, we were very thankful to have learned this, for in our ministry in Spain we didn't want to make assumptions about people. Instead, we wanted to approach each person with an open heart as we guided them to be Christ-followers.

❁

I LEARNED MANY practical pastor's-wife things during those years in Ewing. It seemed that only women could clean the church building and they were expected to dress appropriately while they worked. One summer when members decided that the church needed a thorough cleaning, the women made plans to wash windows, pews, and everything else that was washable. It was decided that I – as the youngest woman on the cleaning crew – would wash windows, so I climbed up on my ladder on that hot, sticky day. I was working hard when I felt a hand go up and down my leg and heard Mrs. Sibley say, "Mrs. McNeely, where are your stockings?" I explained that I always wore stockings to church – except when I was cleaning the building. Her response was, "They have some good cotton ones down at the store. You can't see through them." Ewing, Kentucky, may not have been on a par with Virginia Intermont College but it certainly had its rules for ladies.

While I was on my perch cleaning windows, I witnessed something interesting. As a woman was sweeping the foyer, I saw her look around but not up toward me. Then I saw her lift the corner of the rug and sweep the dirt she had just gathered under it. To this day I've never revealed her name. Even in that first pastorate I was learning that one trait a pastor's wife needs is the ability to keep secrets – small and large.

We loved the people of Ewing Baptist Church and greatly appreciated the hospitality of many fine, supportive people. It was a positive first-experience for a young pastor's wife like me.

❋

FOLLOWING OUR SECOND summer in Ewing, a committee from Mt. Zion Baptist Church in nearby Grant County, Kentucky, asked Gerald to preach one Sunday morning in their new church building. The church then asked him to consider becoming their pastor. As we prayed about the matter, we both clearly felt called to move to that church. The year was 1950.

As one of the largest rural Baptist churches in Kentucky, Mt. Zion was much more active than Ewing had been. As in Ewing, we found the people at Mt. Zion to be dedicated to the Lord.

Even though the area around Mt. Zion offered more opportunity for church growth, it was still country living. On weekends and in the summer months, we lived in the large church parsonage, which was within easy walking distance of the church. (During the school year, we continued to live in Eastwood.) When we moved into the parsonage, it had no running water, so our water came from a nearby cistern. Soon my father – who would tackle anything – built us a large cabinet for the kitchen and Gerald's father bought a hand pump to go on the cabinet, so we could have water in the house. (Of course, we had an outhouse.)

As at Ewing, we had only good experiences at Mt. Zion. Our first daughter was born on July 24, 1951, while we lived there. Linda Susan was the delight of the church. The young people especially loved her – even to the point of putting lipstick on her when she was a wee baby.

Three weeks after Linda's birth in Louisville, I resumed teaching the women's Sunday school class with Linda on a pillow ensconced in the pew in front of me. Then one of the women, Mrs. Barnes, offered to take care of her during class. We could not have found a better caregiver. She loved Linda as if she were her own granddaughter. She even made Linda several dresses and a quilt that became a family treasure.

As a new mother I got plenty of advice on how to rear Linda – and I sometimes overheard other bits of advice. One day I overheard some women arguing about whether the baby's head or feet should be closer to the heater we were using in the church basement. I don't remember which side won, but baby Linda didn't seem to care.

Another time after a women's luncheon meeting at the home of Mrs. D., some of us women were washing dishes and cleaning the kitchen when it came time for me to give Linda her bottle. She'd drunk about half the milk when I put her on my shoulder to burp her. Suddenly Mrs. D. grabbed the bottle and poured the remaining milk down the sink. When I told her that Linda had only drunk half the milk and needed more, she said, "No, you'll just make her sick. Didn't you just hear her burp?" Now, Mrs. D. was very unselfish. She was the only woman in the church who had a driver's license and a car and was always willing to drive everyone anywhere they needed to go. But she had no children. Still, she saw me as a poor young mother who didn't know anything about babies. Fortunately, Linda was satisfied and made no fuss. By the time we got home, she did let me know she was still hungry.

❋

SO MANY PEOPLE at Mt. Zion made significant contributions to our lives. I will only write about a few.

When I think of Mt. Zion Baptist, the first couple who come to mind is Mr. Lonnie and Mrs. Ella Johnson. Although elderly at the time, they continued to be active, both in the church and in the association of Baptist churches of which Mt. Zion was a member. Mrs. Ella had taught children in Sunday school for so long that several younger church members – and some not so young – enjoyed recalling things they'd learned from the lady they called Miss Ella. Mr. Lonnie was the treasurer of the association and had the distinction of having attended the annual meeting of the association more years than anyone else. His parents had taken him to an associational meeting as a baby and he hadn't missed a meeting since.

Don and Fredericka Bingham were two of the lifelong friends we made at Mt. Zion. They owned a farm and liked to entertain large groups. I especially remember an oyster supper at their home. So many church members came that the Binghams had to set up an extra table in the living room. (I also remember that the Binghams were the only family in the church with indoor plumbing.) After we moved to Spain, we often visited the Binghams when we were back in the States on furlough. In 2015, their daughters, Garlene and Grace Ella, remain close friends.

Don's parents were our closest neighbors – and better neighbors never existed. Every Friday during the winter months when we arrived in Mt. Zion after classes at the seminary and my week of teaching school in Simpsonville, Mr. B. always had a fire blazing in our kitchen stove, which meant both the kitchen and the adjoining bedroom were warm. Mrs. Bingham often had a delicious meal prepared for us as well. Most importantly, Gerald and I knew that she prayed for us regularly. Although she never gave us unasked-for advice, she was always ready to answer our questions.

In fact, Mrs. B. was the first person I told about the feeling I had as a twelve-year-old that God wanted me to do something special with my life and about His definite call to me many years later to be a foreign missionary. (By that time, Gerald and I had moved from Mt. Zion to serve another church. I will write about that later in this chapter.) I told her that for Gerald it was a non-issue because he knew we both were committed to whatever the Lord wanted. I told her that to that point, nothing had directed us definitively toward missions. We both strongly believed that God would lead us step by step and while we both were always listening, a call to missions hadn't come. I also told her that since God was blessing our ministry in the pastorate, I must have been mistaken. Mrs. Bingham said she would pray for us and that if God wanted us to be missionaries, both of us would know it. A few years later, God answered her prayers. We were so blessed that she continued to pray for us the rest of her life.

Another special couple was Mr. and Mrs. Ray Lawrence. Their son Raymond was also a student at Southern Seminary, and he and his wife, Eula, were our dear friends. One night all four of us were staying with the elder Lawrences when what came to be known as "The Big Snow" fell. That night, church member Jane Points called to ask if Mr. Lawrence could take Gerald and me to her house in his farm truck. It seems that her daughter's boyfriend was going to have to spend the night there because of the snow, and they wanted Gerald and me there, too. I guess it was to keep things above board.

Mr. Lawrence thought his truck could make it through the snow with no problem and so we set out. We arrived safely and were in time to eat supper with the Points. I remember that we had an angel food cake that Mrs. Points had baked especially for me.

Many years later when we were serving in Spain, Jane left some money for us in her will. At the time, we were planning to buy a piano and had settled on the one we could afford, although it wasn't the one we really wanted. The money Jane left us allowed us to buy a much better piano. I'm not sure when she made her will, but I imagine she was smiling as she thought about how we'd helped her out by doing a small favor during a big snowstorm.

❁

DURING OUR TWO summers at Mt. Zion the girls in my Sunday school class spent a lot of time at our house. Sometimes they came over for advice or just to talk. They shared things with me that they didn't feel they could share with anyone else. Some of their parents thought I should just send them home, but both Gerald and I believed their presence in our home provided extra teaching moments. The fact that they wanted to spend time with us also showed their love for us, love which we gladly returned. One of the girls even made a dress for Linda. After she wore it that summer, we saved it. Linda later used it to dress one of her dolls. In 2015, she still has it.

Many, many years later after we had retired and moved back to Kentucky from Spain, the youngest girl in that class called us to say that she and her husband were coming to Louisville for the day and wanted to take Gerald and me out to eat. That day, they treated us to a wonderful steak dinner in one of the best restaurants in Louisville.

Another of those girls – now a grandmother in 2015 – recently wrote us to say that she has never forgotten those days when she and the other girls came to our house. She wrote me to say, "When someone is so patient with young people like that, it's never forgotten." Funny thing, I don't remember being patient; I just remember how much I loved those kids.

Gerald had his own special ministry with some of the boys in the church. When he heard that some of them were having trouble with their schoolwork, he suggested they come to our home after school so he could help them. When the weather was cold, we always kept a fire going in the stove in the dining room so it would be comfortable for them as they worked around our dining room table. Many years later when we visited

Mt. Zion Church, we saw some of those same boys who had grown up to be leaders in the church.

Shortly after we retired in 1990, Gerald was asked to preach in a morning worship service at Mt. Zion. Soon after the service had concluded, he had a heart attack. Several adults who had been among our youth when Gerald had been pastor skipped their Thanksgiving dinners that day to take us to the hospital. After treatment at the local hospital, we were told to go to a larger hospital in Covington. Those now-grown-up youth stayed by my side until Gerald was admitted. One of those youth, Dorothy Jane, even rode with me in the ambulance with Gerald. She then went back to the church and picked up our car and drove it to the hospital. Throughout that frightening experience, those youth were there for us. Later Gerald wrote to thank them for all they had done that day. Still later one of the women said that after her husband died, she had found Gerald's note in his Bible.

❧

I READILY ADMIT that I felt spoiled at Mt. Zion. Many women in other churches we served cooked foods that Gerald especially liked, but several women at Mt. Zion baked angel food cakes just for me. Mrs. Mullins was one of those dear ladies. Since her house was set a short distance back from the road, she would send her daughter Ida Mae down the road with a cake. In 2015, more than sixty years later, Ida Mae is still one of my best friends. She belongs to a Bible study group that regularly sent Gerald, our girls, and me gifts while we served in Spain. Even in 2015, the group sends Gerald and me a card about once a month to remind us that they are praying for us. Ida Mae's sister Emma Lou was a special friend until her death, too.

Looking back, I often wonder why it's important to remember such things. I think it's because we built such strong relationships with such faithful friends. Their constancy in prayer support and in writing us letters during our years in Spain is something that we will never forget. During difficult times, we often remembered that they were faithfully lifting us up in prayer. That gave us the courage to continue.

❧

AS MUCH AS WE LOVED the people at Mt. Zion Baptist Church, after two years there we knew God was calling us to accept the pastorate of Carlisle Baptist Church, about forty miles northeast of Lexington. Many people didn't understand why we would leave a dynamic, growing church to go to what was known as a church in decline. But God was calling and Gerald felt we should answer that call even if we couldn't understand it completely.

I still remember the first sermon Gerald preached at Carlisle Baptist Church. It was based on Exodus 17. In that passage, when Moses held up his hands the battle went in favor of the Israelites and when he could no longer hold up his hands, the battle went in favor of the enemy. So when Moses became tired, a couple of the Israelites held his hands up in order that the battle would continue to go in their favor.

I even remember the comments I heard after church that day. Dr. Cowan, a much beloved dentist in town, said, "That was a sermon of a leader." Others agreed, and the church extended a call for Gerald to be pastor. Under Gerald's leadership, that declining church soon came to life.

Dr. Cowan and his family became our close friends. Their daughter, Virginia, had a daughter about our Linda's age, and the girls became friends, too.

❊

DURING OUR FOUR years in Carlisle, Gerald visited every home in the community. He also offered to pick up people who didn't have transportation to come to church. He had one especially touching experience with two little girls who often rode to church with him. The road in front of their house was very rough, and he mentioned that to them in passing. The next time he went to pick up the girls, they were gathering rocks and trying to repair the road.

God abundantly blessed the church. Sunday school and worship service attendance grew. We also started Baptist Training Union, which met each Sunday night before the evening worship service. Gerald persuaded Eugene Snapp, a man who'd never held a leadership role in the church, to direct this new organization. Eugene not only became an excellent leader but he and his wife, Louise, also became our good friends. It wasn't long before attendance had increased to the point that the church building needed to be enlarged, and that was done.

Gerald and I often opened our home for group meetings in Carlisle, just as we'd done at Mt. Zion. The parsonage was really a dream. Everything had been freshly painted and papered before we moved in. With the help of family and friends, we'd been able to furnish it well. And it had indoor plumbing. A few years later, all the furnishings that had been so lovingly assembled were sold when we moved to Spain.

❁

OUR SECOND DAUGHTER, Marsha Ellen, was born July 01, 1955, while we were serving at Carlisle. Marsha was the delight of the church, just as Linda had been at Mt. Zion. The members felt she belonged to them. Marsha was a good excuse to revive the church nursery and enlist wonderful people to work there. Linda was too old for the nursery, so I would sit with her on the back pew. That served two purposes: to keep Linda entertained with paper and crayons and to look over the congregation to see if there were any new people or to determine who was absent.

One time Linda got away from me during a prayer and crawled under the pews and past people's feet until she reached the front of the church. Gerald was singing a solo at the time, so Linda went to stand beside him and put her arm around his leg. She enjoyed the attention she was getting and peeked around at people in the congregation. As soon as I could, I retrieved her and took her outside to sit on the front step with me. Before I could say a word, she began to cry. I reminded her that she had hurt her Daddy and his song. Soon we were ready to return to our pew. She never tried that trick again.

❁

IN 1950, WHILE we were still serving at Mt. Zion I'd enrolled in Southern Seminary in Louisville. Since I knew that God had called me to full-time Christian service – meaning a full-time vocation in church work – I wanted to be as prepared as possible. At the time, many Southern Baptist women across the country aspired to attend the Woman's Missionary

Union Training School at Southern Seminary – the school had been established in 1907 specifically to train women for Christian missions and ministry.

In a class that had focused on the role of Woman's Missionary Union (WMU) in the local church, an instructor had said that as a rule it was better that the pastor's wife not be president of the church organization. He said it was better for the pastor's wife to be a youth leader. I had liked that, because I loved working with youth.

Now at Carlisle, I expected to work with youth – until church leaders suggested that I become WMU president. They said the organization had become stale and they thought I would bring life to it. And so, in spite of what I'd been taught, I accepted. Little did I know how WMU would become a vital part of my ministry in later years.

Because I wasn't going to be youth leader, I knew I needed to find someone competent to lead the youth. Dorothy Neal, who was a home demonstration agent and a leader in the community, accepted the position. When she came to our home to discuss it, we also talked about the new house she and her husband, Eugene, were building. As we talked about the furniture she planned to use, suddenly she said, "Yes, these things will be very convenient and I do look forward to the new house, but I would give up all of that for one thing you have." She told me that she and Eugene were sad that they might never have children. Already, they loved our Linda and she loved them in return. Linda loved calling Eugene by his middle name – Swango – and he loved calling her by her middle name – Susan. Little did I know how much the Neals would be involved in Linda's life and in our lives over the years.

We turned to the Neals when Gerald and I felt God's call to missionary service about four years later and began preparations for going to Spain. We were required to attend Foreign Mission Board orientation in Texas but couldn't take our daughters with us, and so we asked Dorothy and Eugene to keep Linda while we were away. (Marsha stayed with friends in Louisville.) When we returned from Texas and went to pick up Linda, we found her and Eugene lying on their stomachs coloring in a coloring book he and Dorothy had bought for her. Linda acted glad to see us and then got on her tricycle and started riding around and around the Neal's beautiful antique dining room furniture. When we tried to get her to stop,

Dorothy and Eugene just laughed at us. They had gone to our house while we were away to pick up the tricycle and they intended for Linda to use it.

Many years later when Linda returned from Spain to attend college in Mississippi, Dorothy and Eugene told her to make their Kentucky home her own. As surrogate parents, they were just what a lonely girl needed. When Linda transferred to Georgetown College, she was only a few miles from Carlisle and spent many weekends with the Neals. Dorothy taught her to cook and sew. She also taught Linda how to arrange flowers and some basics of gardening.

Still later when Linda was planning her wedding, Dorothy encouraged her to make her own wedding dress. She paid for the fabric and told Linda that if she made a mistake cutting into the satin, not to worry because "there was more where that came from". Dorothy and her sister even traveled to Louisville to decorate the church and the reception table for the wedding.

Much later still Linda returned the love the Neals had shown her when Dorothy – who was a widow by then – was temporarily moved to a rehab facility in Lexington to recover from a stroke. She was too weak and too sick to feed herself, so Linda fed her when she visited. When Dorothy returned to her home in Carlisle, she required constant care. Sometime in those years Linda also bought a collection of dolls that she knew Dorothy liked and gave them to her, one on each visit.

Before Dorothy had gone to the rehab facility in Lexington, Linda took me to visit her in Carlisle. By then she was bedridden. When she saw Linda, her face lit up. When she saw me, however, she just stared as though trying to decide who I was. That day I thought back to the time so many years before when Dorothy had told me how precious my children were. It seemed Dorothy and Eugene had gotten a daughter after all.

❁

AS IN OUR PREVIOUS churches, we made deep, personal life-long friendships and precious memories at Carlisle. As in the other two churches, these constant and devoted friends lifted us during our years in Spain. They prayed for us, wrote to us, and often provided things we needed in our ministry. And they did special things, as well. For example, every year we were at Carlisle, Lucille Stone made us a jam cake. Then after we moved to Spain, each time we came to Kentucky on furlough, one of her "traveling jam cakes" would be packed in our luggage when we returned to Spain. Linda has continued the jam cake tradition and makes one using Lucille's recipe every year for her daddy's birthday.

At Carlisle we had really good neighbors, too, in spite of the fact that Tommy, the youngest child of the family next door, cried a lot. One day I spanked Linda for something. (Maybe that was the time she cut Marsha's hair as they both were sitting under the dining room table while I was on the phone. She then put Marsha's curls in her fuzzy house slippers.) Anyway, Linda began to cry. That didn't last long because we heard Tommy begin to cry next door. Linda went to the open window and in a perfectly normal voice said, "Don't cry Tommy, I'm crying now." She began to cry again, making the most of it, though without any real tears.

❀

IT WAS WHILE we were serving at Carlisle that I received my definite call to missions. One night as I was speaking at a banquet for young women from several Baptist churches around Maysville, Kentucky, I asked the women, "Are you sure you are in God's will?" Then a strange feeling came over me. That led me to ask the women again, "Are you really sure you are in God's will?" That time, a voice seemed to say to me, "June, are you sure *you* are in God's will?" That question to me was so real that I stopped speaking for a minute.

On the way home one of the women in the car asked me if I was feeling alright because I was unusually quiet. "You are usually talking on these trips," she said. She didn't know that I was talking to God. I was saying something like this, "Lord, if I heard You correctly – as I'm sure I did – remember I have a husband and two little girls. What do I do about that? If You really want me to go (be a missionary overseas), then You had better tell Gerald, too. You know I can't abandon my little ones." You see, by that time I was a wife, mother of two girls ages five and almost two, a pastor's wife, a school teacher, and a student at The Southern Baptist Theological Seminary in Louisville. How, I wondered, could I become a missionary?

When I got home, I didn't tell Gerald about what I had experienced. I wanted him to experience the same call I had without being influenced by me. I wanted to wait to see how God would lead.

As God would have it, that same week our church was hosting a week-long World Missions Conference in which Southern Baptist missionaries who were serving in different parts of the world spoke at the services. I, however, wasn't able to attend, because both of our girls had chicken pox. So I stayed home with them and prayed.

One night that week when Gerald got home from church, he asked me a question: "What would you think if I told you I have a feeling God is telling us He wants us to be foreign missionaries?" I simply said, "Let's pray about it." God had taken care of my concerns. I had waited and prayed. As soon as Gerald told me what he was feeling, I told him what had happened to me when I had been speaking to those women. Now Gerald and I were on the same page. We began the process to be appointed as Southern Baptist foreign missionaries. Soon we both knew that God had plans for us – including leaving Carlisle Baptist Church, a church we had come to love dearly.

At last, our dear Mrs. Bingham's prayers were to be answered. Gerald and I were sure God wanted us on some foreign mission field. But where? Only He knew.

And everyone who has left houses or brothers or sisters
or father or mother or children
for my sake
will receive a hundred times as much
and will inherit eternal life.
Matthew 19:29

FIVE

❁

O ur call from God had been confirmed and we had said, "Yes." Gerald and I were going to be missionaries. We immediately called the Southern Baptist Foreign Mission Board (FMB; in 2015, the International Mission Board) located in Richmond, Virginia, only to learn that the Director of Personnel was visiting his parents who lived near Carlisle, where we were currently living. He came to see us right away.

We asked him two questions: "Is this real?" followed by "Where are we most needed?" He told us that the greatest need that fit our qualifications was at the *Seminario Teológico Bautista* (Spanish Baptist Seminary) in Barcelona, Spain. As God would have it, the school needed a New Testament professor. At that time, in addition to his pastoral duties at Carlisle Baptist, Gerald was teaching New Testament at an extension of Campbellsville (KY) College (now University) located in Maysville. It seemed a perfect fit. The personnel director asked us to continue to pray about specifically going to Spain and to fill out some preliminary forms.

Even before we'd met with the personnel director, we'd already been praying for the seminary. We'd met the seminary director (president) Roy Wyatt and his wife, Joyce, in Louisville while they were on a short furlough. In our brief visit with them, they had asked us to pray for the seminary but hadn't told us about the need for a New Testament professor. They'd also told us that their son Mike was going to be in first grade in a private Swiss School in Barcelona when they returned to Spain. "Why is he not in a local public school?" we'd wondered. "Will we need to place our children in a private school?" Joyce had told us something else that we didn't understand: she had a helper in her home. "Why is that necessary?" we'd asked ourselves. "Can't she handle the housework herself? How could housekeeping be more complicated in Spain than in the U.S.? Would my (June's) missionary work make having a helper necessary?" After that conversation with the Wyatts, we knew we had much to learn about Spain, and we began seeking answers.

❊

BUT FIRST WE HAD to tell our families and our church about our decision. Thankfully, our families accepted the news well. They – like the people at Carlisle church – knew we were following God's leading even though we would miss them and they would miss us. Mother's heart was always tender toward missions, so she wasn't surprised. She had always wanted us to do God's will. As for Dad, as usual he said little, but we knew he was proud of us.

Gerald's parents were a little more surprised and sad about our going than my parents were; nevertheless, they supported our decision as God's will. Gerald's dad even promised to send us the Louisville *Courier-Journal* newspaper from time to time – which he did once a week for several years. He would remove all advertising and then send us the daily comic strips and articles that he thought we might enjoy. Gerald's mom was the most surprised of all our parents, but she was encouraging and happy for us.

When we told Mr. Reynolds, who had been my attorney-boss and mentor in high school, he was very excited about our decision. From time to time over the years, he included a check in his letters to us.

We knew we had to find a special way to let our girls know that we were leaving our Carlisle home, church, and friends. And so we held hands with almost-two-year-old Marsha and almost-six-year-old Linda and prayed that God would bless us as a family as He had blessed our pastoral ministry. Marsha was too young to understand, but Linda had just finished a missions study on Japan in Sunbeams (a Baptist missions organization for preschoolers) and replied to our news by saying, "Maybe God wants *you* to go to Spain, but He wants *me* to go to Japan!"

We explained that God really wanted her to go to Spain with us. We told her that when she got older He might want her to go to Japan. We told her we could all pray for Japan even though we would be living in Spain. That almost satisfied her. Still, she took the prayer for Japan very seriously. One day as we were walking on Fourth Street in downtown Louisville, we saw a small picture of a Japanese scene. Linda was drawn to it immediately. We told her that if we bought it, it could remind us to pray for Japan. When we got to Spain, the picture hung over her bed for a long time. Later it hung in our breakfast room. It did remind us to pray for Japan.

The Sunday we told the good people at Carlisle church that we were leaving, Gerald decided to make a home movie, so everyone went outside the building and Gerald filmed the people re-entering the church. There were many tears to join ours. Even in 2015, I can see Edna Cowan as she passed Gerald with tears in her eyes and shook her fist at us. We knew we could count on the prayers of the Cowan family.

❁

"WHY SPAIN?" "Isn't Spain a Catholic country? "Aren't Catholics Christian?" When we told other people about our decision, they often responded with those questions. And, honestly, we were asking ourselves those same questions. At first, it was hard for us to understand the finer points separating Spanish Catholicism from American Catholicism until we were reminded that Jesus had said, "The field is the world" (Matthew 13:38) – that included Spain.

We learned that the Spanish government had absolute control over all areas of Spanish life – even matters of personal faith – and that Catholicism was forced by the government. We learned that Dictator Francisco Franco had often said, "Spain is, always has been, and always will be a Roman Catholic country." We learned that evangelical churches only had the right to exist if they had been established prior to the Civil War that began in 1936 – it was now 1957. And even if evangelical churches did exist, they did so with severe restrictions. As Americans, that was hard for even Gerald and me to grasp – much less others with whom we talked. We were all so accustomed to the freedoms we enjoyed in the States. Gerald and I were totally unfamiliar with an imposed state religion. It wouldn't be long, however, before we'd know from personal experience what that means.

We also learned that in Spain every adult was required to carry a citizen's card with his or her picture on it. Since we wouldn't be Spanish citizens, we learned that we'd be required to carry our passports at all times and get a residency card. (I'll write more about that in chapter nine.)

❀

IN SPITE OF – as well as because of – what we were learning, Gerald and I still definitely felt called to Spain. We felt our gifts, our backgrounds, our education, and our experiences in the three churches where we had served in Kentucky were the Lord's doing. Each place we'd served had been important in His kingdom work. Also, by then Gerald had completed a master of divinity degree and a master of theology degree. In *Seminario Teológico Bautista* (Spanish Baptist Seminary) he would be helping to train pastors to work in about fifty Baptist churches and mission points across the country. We both felt Gerald could make a significant contribution there. As for me, I wasn't sure what I would be doing, but I was secure in knowing that God would show me the way.

A few weeks after we had met with the FMB personnel director, we were invited to go to FMB headquarters in Richmond, Virginia. There we attended meetings with heads of committees who had to approve our appointment as missionaries. We learned practical things such as how to request passports and how to pack. As it turned out, our packing was simple – we couldn't take furniture to Spain because we would be entering as tourists. Also, Spain was just beginning to manufacture home furnishings and didn't allow any foreign home furnishings to enter the country; they didn't want competition. The exceptions were washing machines and refrigerators, which they still didn't manufacture. We learned we would live in a furnished apartment.

We also were told that Spain was still recovering from the terrible civil war that had lasted from 1936 to 1939 and in which more than 500,000 people had been killed. Even after almost twenty years, many people were still living in poverty.

❀

WHEN WE RETURNED to Kentucky from Richmond, we began final preparations for our voyage to Spain. Our mission board gave us suggestions about what we needed to take with us. We gathered theology books and children's books – including World Book Encyclopedia and Childcraft that the girls practically wore out over the next years. We bought and packed enough clothing and shoes for our family to last for the next five years. Working from the list the board had sent us gave us confidence that we were prepared.

Because we couldn't take our household things with us, we had to dispose of them. Being a sentimental person, it was difficult for me to get rid of the things that we had lovingly acquired in ten years of marriage. The Lord knew that, and so just before we retired thirty-three years later, two pieces found their way back to us. Linda was visiting the Neals in Carlisle when Dorothy said she'd found something that had belonged to us. She'd been rummaging around in an antique shop that had opened at the edge of town and had found the pie crust table that had sat between the two windows in our living room in the Carlisle parsonage. By that time, the table had been stripped and refinished and looked wonderful.

When Dorothy had told the antique dealer the story of the table, the woman had said, "You know, I'm pretty sure I have the lamp that went on that table up in the loft," and had proceeded to climb a ladder to get it. Sure enough, it was our lamp. That lamp and table were waiting for us when we returned to Louisville.

Our Board advised us to arrive in New York City a few days before we were scheduled to sail for Spain as there were many things to be rechecked and reconfirmed. We also needed to exchange our American dollars for Spanish *pesetas*. While we were in New York, we were blessed to hear Billy Graham speak at a crusade in Madison Square Garden. For the girls and me, that was the largest arena we'd ever been in. During the service we kept the girls busy with toys and books and then Marsha fell asleep on her daddy's lap. All in all, it was a perfect moment right before setting sail.

Have I not commanded you?
Be strong and courageous.
Do not be terrified;
do not be discouraged,
for the LORD your God will be with you
wherever you go.
Joshua 1:9

Six

❀

Seasoned travelers might have found an ocean voyage aboard a small passenger ship to be an adventure, but for the McNeely family at first the high waves coupled with the Excaliber's size proved to be a bad combination. We definitely knew we were aboard a destination ship, not a luxury cruise liner.

Until they got their sea legs, both Linda and Marsha were sick. Even I had to admit to bouts of queasiness. (Linda remembers the ship moving "a lot" during the first days.) I knew I had to keep going in order to take care of the girls, and so I did. And, yes, even Gerald was seasick in spite of having served in the U.S. Navy. After that voyage, I told the three of them I wanted to be the only one of our family to get seasick on our next trans-Atlantic voyage, so that I could be waited on. As best we remember, no one got sick on those voyages, so that never happened.

As to Gerald's seasickness, I think it was the result of inactivity because when he learned about a Ping-Pong tournament on board, he fully recovered. There's something about knocking a ball back and forth that has appealed to him from the time he was ten years old. In fact, even in 2015 at age 90, he plays tennis regularly. As for that shipboard tournament, Gerald won and became an instant shipboard celebrity. No more seasickness for him.

On that voyage, the very few children on board were only allowed to eat in the dining room at the early children's seating. Rather than eat then, Gerald and I chose to feed the girls in our stateroom, put them to bed, and then go to the dining room for a later seating. We were assured by our steward that the girls would be safe since our stateroom was near the dining room. He said he'd let us know if there were any problems. Of course, there were none. Every night when we returned from dinner, the girls were sound asleep.

In time, our girls found the ship's playroom. Over the next days, Marsha spent long periods there pretending to drive a ship. Actually, the two-year-old was convinced that she was driving the Excaliber. One day when a steward asked her if she'd driven the ship that morning, she happily said that she had. "I thought it was you," he replied. "The ship started going around and around in circles." That made Marsha even surer that she had actually driven the Excaliber. She loved driving the ship so much that sometimes we had to insist that she let other children have a turn. There was also a children's library in the playroom, and the girls kept us reading books to them – that is, when they weren't seasick.

❧

AFTER TEN DAYS at sea, we all were ready for dry land. And so, on Sept. 02, 1957, for the first time we saw Spain, the country where Gerald and I would spend almost three and a half decades and our girls would live until they left for college in the States.

As the Excaliber approached the Barcelona harbor shortly after dawn, we were surprised to see a large group of people waiting for us on the dock. Fellow missionaries Roy and Joyce Wyatt, whom we had met in the U.S.; Russell and Patsy Hilliard, who had arrived in Spain a short time before; and Joe and Lila Mefford were there. Several Spanish pastors and their wives from Baptist churches in Barcelona also had come to welcome us: Don Pedro Bonet and his wife, Doña Noemi; Don Samuel Rodrigo and his family; and Don Luis Hombre. One pastor, Don Felio Simon, had come two hours by train from Manresa. All the women kissed our girls and me on both cheeks, making their warm welcome real for us in true Spanish fashion. (For an explanation of the use of names and honorifics, see Appendix 1.)

Several Spanish women also were in the welcoming party, including Señora Salvadó, who had brought her two little girls, Ani and Mari Salvadó, with her. Marsha and the two girls soon become close friends, so much so that the girls came to meet our ship or plane every time we returned from stateside furlough over the next years.

Of course, we didn't know what the Spanish Christians in the group were saying to us since we didn't know a word of Spanish, so the Meffords and the Wyatts translated. The Hilliards also benefited from the translations since they hadn't been in Spain long enough to learn Spanish. Charles and Indy Whitten were the only other Southern Baptist missionaries assigned to Spain at the time, but they were on stateside furlough. The Meffords, the Wyatts, the Hilliards, the Whittens, and Gerald and I were the total Southern Baptist missionary force in Spain in 1957.

That morning the Wyatts took us to their home for breakfast. During the meal they told us that we were the answer to their prayers for the seminary. Gerald and I had prayed for something specific, too, and that day we got our answer. We had prayed that God would give us a confirmation that we were where He wanted us to serve. When we saw how well we were received – not just by those who were now our missionary colleagues, but also by the Spanish Christians – we knew we had our answer.

We also had prayed that our girls would have friends. That prayer was answered as well. The Wyatts' son, Mike, was Linda's age, and both of them would be in the same school. Their daughter, Anita, was a couple of years older than Marsha, but they played together well that day. The Mefford children – Sylvia, Tony, and Janie – also seemed to be glad to have two more MK (Missionary Kid) cousins as they welcomed our girls with enthusiasm. In fact, over the next months, as the Mefford children and our girls got to know each other, two-year-old Marsha became especially fond of Tony, who was about seven or eight. She liked to follow him around, holding his hand and calling him "my boy". Tony was unbelievably patient with her.

❃

FOR OUR FIRST night in Spain, the Meffords had reserved a place for us in the *pensión* (a small hotel or rooming house) where they were staying in Barcelona. Our first experience with Spanish food and customs came that night when dinner was served at 9 p.m. – which we learned was the typical dinner hour. In fact, most restaurants didn't even open until 9 p.m.

That night, dinner began with a first *plato*, a plate of unseasoned green beans. Cruets of olive oil and vinegar, salt, and other condiments were on the table so that we could dress the beans to our taste. The beans were followed by a meat course and then by fruit that we peeled ourselves. Lila explained that sweets were served only on special occasions and that fruit was the typical last course.

That night, our family slept in one room on a bed and two small cots. The mattresses were filled with straw and the sheets were so coarse that some of the straw poked through and scratched Marsha's face. The bathroom was the size of a small closet. Plus, we were given just one towel for the four of us. When I asked the housekeeper for an extra one, she said she'd try to find one, which she did.

❋

THE MEFFORDS HAD found a furnished apartment on the fourth floor of an eight-story building on Calle Balmes (Balmes Street) for us to consider, so on our first day in Barcelona Joe took us to see it. When the owner came to the door, Joe explained why we'd come. She said, "Wait just a minute," and closed the door. Another lesson in Spanish culture had begun. Joe explained that no Spanish *señora* would ever be seen in public in a house dress. We didn't have long to wait. When she returned, she graciously invited us in. She not only had changed clothes but also had availed herself of the pretty vanity in the master bedroom and put on makeup, including lipstick.

We immediately fell in love with the apartment. It was so lovely we felt sure it was far too luxurious for us. It had a pretty *entrada* (foyer) used to receive guests. Many times, this was the only spot visitors saw. In the foyer were a chest of drawers and some attractive chairs. The living room and dining room were also pretty with dark green velvet furnishings. Between the living and dining rooms, we saw pocket doors that could be opened for entertaining large groups. Little did we know that we would need that extra space when American 6th Fleet ships were in port and we would entertain many sailors. From tables to lamps to the size of the apartment, everything seemed far too fine for us.

In the master bedroom, there was a little alcove between two windows with that gorgeous dressing table that any woman would want. The girls' room had two twin beds and a wardrobe. We checked the mattresses: They were wool, not straw like the ones we'd slept on in the *pensión* the night before. (We would learn that those woolen mattresses had to be beaten and fluffed regularly.) Another room that we would use as a guest room and a playroom for the girls had a three-quarter bed. Little did we know how many overnight guests would sleep in that bed.

The apartment also had a small bedroom and bath designed for a live-in helper. We soon learned such an apartment was typical in all but the most humble homes in Spain.

The rental price was unusually low and within what the FMB allowed, so we agreed to take it. On our first day in Spain, we moved in – after all, we only had two trunks and some suitcases.

The only large items we had shipped from the States were a refrigerator and wringer washing machine, and we eagerly awaited their arrival. Neither ever arrived. We learned that they had made it to the Barcelona port, but for some unknown reason couldn't clear customs. Eventually, they ended up in Rhodesia (now Zimbabwe). Several months later we were able to buy a refrigerator and washing machine from some Americans who were returning to the U.S.

In the meantime I didn't know what to do about our laundry, so I asked Joyce Wyatt for advice. She said that our helper would take care of that. Helper? Yes, we would have a helper. Joyce showed me a large, built-in concrete tub with a rough side that served as a washboard. I wondered how long our clothes would last with that treatment, but Spanish families used them and so would we. Joyce also showed me the clothes line outside the kitchen window where our helper would hang the washed clothes. It was a dreary sight. Looking up and down and all around us from our window, I could see clothes hanging from the windows of other apartments. Two floors up on the sixth floor, I seemed to see a shaft where a little sunlight could shine on the laundry.

The bathroom had a hot water heater so it had hot water, but the kitchen didn't have a hot water heater – which meant there was no hot water there. When I asked the owner if a hot water heater could be installed in the kitchen, she asked, "Why?" With the help of translator Joe, I told her that I liked to wash dishes in hot water. She looked at me as if to say, "*Esos Americanos locos.*" Translation: "Those crazy Americans." She later agreed we could put one in at our expense. Roy Wyatt, who was always wonderful to help and solve problems, took charge of all the details.

Until our refrigerator arrived, we planned to use the small icebox in the kitchen that would at least hold milk and butter. On our first night in the apartment, Gerald woke to find water on the kitchen floor and surrounding areas. It seemed that the holding pan that was supposed to collect water as the ice melted had a crack in it. Until we could have the pan repaired, we simply set the alarm clock each night when we went to bed and woke up to the 2 a.m. alarm and emptied the melted ice. To have the pan repaired required communication skills we didn't yet have, and we had to wait for Roy's assistance. In addition to being director/president of the seminary, he was kept busy with handling the details of life in Spain by our family and the Hilliards, who also were new to the country. Finally, Roy had time to have the pan welded, and we were in business.

Without a refrigerator, we had to learn how to procure ice. The owner of the apartment explained that we could put a sign on our little balcony that said, *Hielo* (ice). When the iceman saw the sign, he would come up to our apartment and bring ice. Until we could arrange that, Gerald often saw a very dignified Roy Wyatt – dressed in a nice suit – walking up the street with a block of ice for our little icebox.

Looking back, perhaps the best thing about the apartment was its location, steps from the subway (Metro) stop, two Metro stations from the Swiss School our girls would attend, and within walking distance of Bona Nova Baptist Church and the seminary. At one store along the way, we found our first purchase in Spain – a beautiful demitasse set. We'd been told that such a set was a necessity in Spain, and we soon learned that was true. Now, in 2015, that coffee set belongs to Marsha. I wanted her to have it since she helped me choose it.

Linda and Marsha soon adjusted to their new surroundings. They, however, were afraid when their daddy was away from home. Their room was directly across from the front door and that unsettled them, so we installed a chain on the door and found them a plaque that read, "Jesus said, 'I am with you always.'" That seemed to make them relax and let them sleep.

From the beginning, we all adjusted well to apartment living, which was good because over the next thirty-three years, several apartments would be our home. Actually, we found the close living quarters in apartment buildings helped us to meet our neighbors more easily than if we had lived in free-standing houses. Hearing our neighbors through thin walls became a part of the experience and never bothered us very much.

❁

AT LAST WE WERE MISSIONARIES. I remember thinking how, step by step, things were already falling into place. Our apartment was within walking distance of our work and our church. It was also within easy access to the school our girls would attend. We had just moved into our nice apartment. We had been warmly greeted by those people with whom we would work so closely. What more could we ask?

Yes, I still had many unanswered questions, but for now I was open to the adventure and to watching other things fall into place. I was being obedient.

❁

AS FOR A LIVE-IN HELPER, before we'd arrived Joyce Wyatt had asked around for one whom we could hire at the usual salary of 600 *pesetas* per month. We couldn't imagine someone working for such a low sum since at the time 60 *pesetas* converted to one dollar, so we decided to pay our first helper 700 pesetas instead. As was customary, we would also be responsible for her room and board and occasional tips. We were also to give her at least two uniforms, shoes for housework, and her social security payments.

As it turned out, giving our first helper 700 *pesetas* was a mistake because the helpers in the other apartments in the building soon learned about it and asked that their salaries be raised to keep up with those *"Americanos locos."* Gerald and I had much to learn about Spanish domestic practices.

Our first helper had never worked in a home before. On her first day with us, she seemed fascinated with our laundry tub with the washboard side. When she did the laundry for the first time she gathered all the linens and clothing she could find – whether dirty or clean – and started a big washing. It was simply too much for her, so she gave up and went home. The next day her mother came with her and finished the washing, hanging it on the four lines outside our kitchen window. She then went around our apartment, showing her daughter what was expected of her. The girl must have been overwhelmed because she never came back. Within a couple of days, we had a new helper.

Traditionally, a helper's responsibilities included cooking and cleaning and taking care of the children in the household. I, however, loved to cook, so I did the cooking. I did ask our helper to assist with the time-consuming grocery shopping since one had to go to the market daily (no packaged foods) and had to go from store to store to purchase the things we needed (no supermarkets). Grocery shopping could take hours. Our helper also cared for Marsha every afternoon while I was in Spanish class or at work at the seminary library.

We employed a helper for several years until costs rose beyond what we felt we could pay. Looking back, in those early years I could never have devoted myself to intensive language study or have carried out my responsibilities of running a library and teaching in the seminary as quickly as I did without having a helper. Daily living tasks would have been incredibly time consuming and left little time for anything else.

❀

AS WE SETTLED INTO our new home, we discovered an unexpected delight. Every Sunday afternoon when it wasn't raining various groups met in the plaza outside our window and held hands to form circles to dance the *Sardana*, the beautiful dance of the region of Cataluña performed either in three–quarter or five–eighth time. Accompanied by reed instruments, Spaniards of all generations gathered to dance that regional dance, even though doing so had been declared illegal. We also learned that speaking the language of Cataluña – Catalán – was against the law. In spite of everything, each week the dancers seemed never to tire of dancing. We never tired of watching, the four of us standing on our tiny balcony off the dining room.

That was just one of the many delightful experiences we enjoyed as we got to know Barcelona in our first months there. There was much to explore in a city suited to pedestrians and with excellent public transportation. We quickly learned the Metro (subway) and learned to navigate the narrow streets and wide, tree-shaded avenues.

In 1957, Barcelona was a busy city of about 2.5 million people. Mopeds, bicycles, electric cable cars, and the Metro were the means of transportation. Mopeds – many with sidecars that were often packed with family members – filled the streets. Men in suits with briefcases in tow rode bicycles to work. Electric cable cars crisscrossed busy plazas. Within a few years, however, buses, taxis, and personal cars would begin to replace mopeds, bicycles, and cable cars.

After we were able to say a few words and ask some necessary questions in Spanish, the city began to feel like home. Barcelona was beautiful and the people we met were delightful. We felt reassured that this was indeed where God wanted our little family.

When we arrived in 1957, all around us we saw the effects of the slow recovery from the Spanish Civil War that had ended eighteen years earlier. We saw shelled-out buildings standing next to new modern buildings. In those shelled buildings, we saw stairs clinging to the interior walls and could tell which rooms had been children's rooms by the decorations on the walls.

At the same time the Spanish people were trying hard to get back to normal. We discovered florist shops and beauty salons in unexpected places. We knew the people didn't have much money, so we often wondered how they could support those shops. Many times in the market we saw women with a few potatoes and a vegetable or a piece of fruit in their market baskets and on top of those meager purchases would be a small bouquet of flowers. Maybe the flowers were a symbol of promise and expectation. To Gerald and me, it seemed that the city was willing itself to put the horrors of the war behind them and move forward.

Yet, signs of the war were pervasive. We saw many women dressed in black. We learned that some were elderly widows, but many others were women who had lost someone in the Civil War. To symbolize their sorrow, for several years after their loved one had died, they only wore black. Some even wore black for the rest of their lives.

Those not in black, however, dressed in the latest fashions, even though most owned few clothes. Most women, in fact, had only one good dress, but it was always neat and fashionable and was worn whenever she went out and when she entertained guests in her home.

❀

EARLY ON, we were invited into the homes of pastors and laypeople and were always warmly received – and they were very patient with our limited Spanish. No matter how humble the home, it was always clean and in order. One family even showed us their storage room – which was neater than many pantries I'd seen in the States. It wasn't a question of how many possessions you had; rather it was about taking care of what you had.

We also were warmly welcomed as we began to visit the churches. As a family, we thrived on the experiences of making new, dear friends. The people in the churches were always excited and honored to have us visit and always appreciated our encouragement. From the beginning of our time in Spain, we felt the enormous weight of governmental repression that the churches as well as individual Christians carried daily. Their sacrifice was always on our minds.

❀

NOT ONLY WAS SPAIN economically impoverished but it also was ruled by an absolute dictator. Generalíssimo Francisco Franco had controlled every aspect of Spanish life since he'd assumed power in 1939 as the victor in the Civil War. Because news about Spain was still censored in 1957, it was always hard to know what was really going on in the country. Fortunately, Gerald had packed a short-wave radio before we left the States. Over the years, he used it frequently to tune in to the British Broadcasting Company to try to learn what was happening in Spain.

As I wrote in chapter five, Franco often said, "Spain is, always has been, and always will be a Roman Catholic country." We quickly learned first-hand that his version of Catholicism wasn't what we had known in the United States. Under Franco's rule, no other religion except Roman Catholicism had the legal right to exist. Because of that, many restrictions were placed on evangelical – non-Roman Catholic – churches. Even those churches that had existed before the beginning of the Spanish Civil War – and thus were deemed legal – faced restrictions. While most of those pre-war churches were allowed to continue to function, they faced many limitations just as the newer churches did.

The list of restrictions seemed endless. For example, no evangelical church could have a sign on the church building indicating that it was a church. Often windows had to be closed – even in very hot weather – so singing couldn't be heard from the street. Sometimes worshipers actually whispered hymns rather than singing aloud. Following a church service, those in attendance could not "loiter," which might draw attention to the building. Thus, worshipers left a few at a time and didn't congregate outside the building so as not to attract attention.

Franco's cruel hand didn't just reach into corporate church life but it also reached into the lives of individual Christians – literally from the cradle to the grave. Spaniards had no personal rights. At the whim of the government, you can lose your job, your home, or you could be thrown into prison – where you could have no legal representation.

Parents had to have their babies' names approved by a government agent before the births could be registered. Many times, the agent would reject the name the parents had chosen. One couple, for example, wanted to name their new daughter a name that was popular in other European countries. At first, they were denied because the name wasn't a saint's name or a biblical name. When the couple showed that in some versions of the Bible the name was used, it was reluctantly allowed.

Often weddings of evangelicals had to be postponed because the couple had been denied permission to marry. Some couples were engaged for several years before they were finally granted a marriage license.

Children were not allowed to enroll in school if they lacked a baptismal certificate from the Catholic Church. For families in Baptist churches, there wasn't always a private school option, and if there was, it wasn't affordable. We knew some children who were allowed to enroll in a state school but were persecuted for being evangelicals. The story of two little girls especially touched our hearts. One day their teacher told them to come up front before the class as an object lesson. The teacher then said, "These little girls went to that Protestant church in town last summer, so you don't want to play with them, do you?" The answer from all the children was, of course, *"No, maestra."* Translation: "No, teacher."

Many evangelicals lost their jobs when their employers learned they weren't Catholic. Some were expelled from school; others weren't allowed to practice medicine, dentistry, or law. Some were denied teaching posts.

Ordinary citizens had no access to a Bible. In the Catholic churches, the Bibles were chained to the pulpits and had to be interpreted by a priest. By law, Bibles weren't to be carried on the street; to do so was to proselytize. To circumvent that, evangelical men carried their Bibles in briefcases – even if they didn't need a briefcase. Gerald and I often thought it looked like a lot of the members of our Spanish Baptist churches were stylish business men. Women usually carried their Bibles in the bottom of grocery bags – with their groceries on top. Everyone knew full well that the *Guardia Civil* (Civil Guard) armed with bayonets could inspect brief cases and grocery bags at any time, so they made a point of looking inconspicuous. (The Civil Guard was Dictator Franco's personal army and was distinct from the national army and the police force.)

Non-Roman Catholics were denied permission to bury their loved ones in a public cemetery, so some evangelicals were buried in a place outside the cemetery where criminals were also buried. Others were buried on private property. Gerald and I were first made aware of this restriction after a devastating flood in Tarrasa that resulted in many deaths. The funerals held in the public cemetery and the funerals held outside were markedly different. From inside, we could hear wailing and weeping. Outside in the evangelical burial site, while there was sorrow and tears, the scene was quieter, more dignified and marked with the singing of hymns. In spite of the circumstances, family and friends of those being buried there held on to the promise that their loved ones were in a better place and that they would someday be reunited. Shortly after that same flood, a man who had lost his home and family was seen floating on a log, singing, *"No tengo temor, no tengo temor, Jesús me ha prometido, siempre contigo estoy."* Translation: "I have no fear. Jesus has promised never to leave me alone." What a witness!

As Gerald and I began our missionary service in 1957, those were the conditions in Spain. Toward the end of Franco's life, he did seem to lose interest in the evangelical presence in Spain, which resulted in a noticeable easing of restrictions on evangelicals. (At the same time, the Catholic Church in Spain was also experiencing less governmental control.) Still, severe restrictions on evangelicals remained in effect until 1975 when Franco died.

I will lie down and sleep in peace, for you alone,
O LORD, make me dwell in safety.
Psalm 4:8

SEVEN

❀

As soon as we were settled in our apartment in Barcelona, Gerald and I began looking for a school for six-year-old Linda. Because Marsha was only two, our live-in helper and I would be looking after her.

That brought us face to face with some of the restrictions imposed by the Franco regime. Because Linda didn't have an official baptismal certificate from the state church, she couldn't attend a Spanish public school. To be honest, since the school system had been neglected during the civil war and hadn't yet recovered, we didn't find that to be an attractive option.

As we investigated, we learned that in the previous few years Barcelona had seen an influx of Swiss families working for the Nestle Company. These families also had found the state of the Spanish public schools to be discouraging, and as a result they had started *Escuela Suiza de Barcelona*, or the Swiss School. As we investigated further, we learned that while the school did accept students from all countries, the majority of the students were Spanish children whose families wanted a better education option. (In 1957, only a few internationals lived in Barcelona.) We also learned that the school followed a rigorous Swiss curriculum.

And so we enrolled Linda in the Swiss School. With the exception of Spanish class, school work was conducted entirely in German – a language Linda had never even heard spoken before. As for Spanish, she'd heard that language for the first time only a few weeks earlier. All social interactions were either in Spanish or the local language of Catalán. Speaking English was totally out of the picture – not even for a brief translation. Linda learned later that all the teachers knew English but none of them let her know that and none responded to her English. They must have felt that she'd learn better if she were totally immersed in German and Spanish. So when our first grader was learning to read and write, she was learning in German. As for numbers, that had already been taught in kindergarten, but Linda quickly caught up. (Most of the Spanish children had already completed two years of preschool before first grade; Linda had not.)

To make matters worse, her friend and fellow first-grader Mike Wyatt wasn't allowed to talk to her after the first couple of weeks. Her teachers thought this would keep another crutch away from the learning process, lest the two children revert to speaking in English. Couple all that with not ever having attended school before, it's understandable why Linda had many tearful, confusing times that year. For her, first grade seemed to be full of distressful episodes of tears or vomiting.

A further complication arose when it was found out that Linda was a Protestant – a non-Catholic. The Swiss School served families from Switzerland, Belgium, and other countries with Protestant populations, and most of the international students were Protestant, but because the majority of the students were Spanish and Catholic, Protestants were a distinct minority. (Linda remembers that the Protestants met with a teacher who taught Old Testament stories while the Catholic students met to study catechism.)

By Spanish law, every school in Spain was required to have a Catholic priest, which presented another problem for Linda at the Swiss School. The priest there told all the children in the school that they had to ask permission before they could talk to or play with Linda. While the priest had no authority over the non-Catholic students, the intimidation worked. After that, the children seemed to think that Linda had something contagious and that they might catch it! Looking back in 2015, Linda says, "At the very least the children were told that as a Protestant, I was most assuredly going to hell. You have to wonder what children might want to play with another child with a future like that." As children are wont to do, however, that ban became a part of the fascination Linda possessed. Her classmates began to approach her on a dare, and soon they began chatting with her. Over time, she developed some good friendships. Plus, after a few months, she was fluent in Spanish, which helped ease the chasm between her and the other students.

Both Linda and Marsha, when she was a student there. experienced a particular horror at Christmastime each year when a scary Father Christmas – dressed totally in brown in the Swiss tradition – came to each classroom to mete out punishment for students who had been bad. All the students – including Marsha and Linda – trembled with fear as names were read aloud. Classmates who'd misbehaved were then called to the front of the room and were soundly whipped by Father Christmas with thick switches he kept in his pack. By contrast, good children received tangerines. Even though our girls had done nothing wrong, both thought they would surely be among the children who would receive such public and humiliating whippings. (Father Christmas was the school principal in disguise.)

Escuela Suiza de Barcelona was a very good school academically, but it did have some ideas that were foreign to us. The school day began at 8 a.m. and went until 1 p.m. After a mid-day break for lunch and *siesta*, school resumed at 3 and ran until 5. During the *siesta*, children went home to eat the main meal of the day with their families.

Across Spain, students wore a *delantal* (smock) over their clothes to protect them, and that practice was continued at the Swiss School. The smock reached the knees and had sleeves that covered down to the wrists. Even boys wore smocks through fourth grade. Every Friday, students took their smocks home to be laundered; every Monday morning, they took the clean ones back to school. Actually, the smocks were very helpful, as they did a good job of keeping clothes clean especially since the students used ink wells with stylus pens and blotters.

Along with the customary subjects taught in most elementary schools in the States, at the Swiss School girls were also taught needlecrafts. In first grade, they learned to crochet. This was followed in second grade by knitting, and in third by embroidery. (I don't know what special subjects the boys were learning.) In the needlework classes, Linda presented a real problem because she is left handed. Her teachers simply didn't know how to teach these crafts to a left-handed child. In fact, they told her it would be impossible for her to learn. That, however, didn't stop Linda. After a teacher told her to "pretend you're looking into a mirror" as she worked, she gladly took up the challenge – and she prevailed. Her love for needlecrafts, including quilting, continues to this day. (Marsha didn't have Linda's problem as she is right-handed.)

Being left handed presented an even more serious problem when Linda was learning how to write. Her teacher's goal was to prohibit her from using her left hand and to train her to use only her right, "correct" hand. In the school, students sat at double desks, which meant Linda always had a partner. Her teacher told her partner to jab Linda with her elbow if she ever saw her reverting to using her left hand. In handwriting class, Linda often was told to go to the blackboard and write out the assignment – with her right hand, of course –while the other children were at their desks, writing the same assignment in their notebooks.

Unfortunately, Gerald and I didn't know how to deal with this, and it continued until Linda graduated from the school. As a result, Linda began to stutter – in English, Spanish, and German. That was even more embarrassing for her. When we consulted our doctor – who had been trained in England – he agreed there was a definite connection between being forced to write with the right hand and a speech impediment such as stuttering. He, however, said he didn't want to get involved.

Linda spent grades one, two, four, and six at the school. Marsha spent kindergarten and grade two in the Swiss School.

❀

WITH OUR GIRLS settled into a routine, it was time for Gerald and me to begin our missionary work. We knew that our first task would be to learn the language. In fact, FMB first-year missionaries were expected to devote their time to learning the language and to be only minimally involved in ministry. For us, however, that was not to be. When we arrived in 1957, there was so much ministry work that needed to be done across Spain that another plan had been put in place.

That first year – as I wrote in chapter six – Gerald and I weren't the only new missionaries. Russell and Patsy Hilliard had arrived only a few weeks before us, and they, too, were going through their own adjustments. We soon learned that while both Gerald and Russell would need to spend much of their time in language training in preparation to teach and preach, they also would need to get involved in ministry. They would have to hit the ground running.

As for Patsy and me, we thought we'd be focusing on learning the language and on our families. Then seminary president Roy Wyatt changed that. One day, he asked Patsy and me to each choose a task – either working in the seminary nursery or working in the seminary library. I held my breath, waiting for Patsy's response. Then I heard her say, "Since I already have two children and am expecting another, it would seem logical that I work in the nursery. Besides, I don't know anything about libraries." I breathed a "thank you" to God and relaxed. I'd always found such joy and satisfaction in a library that it seemed to be an act of grace that God would let me serve Him as a missionary in a library.

It didn't take long for me to know the wisdom of Joyce Wyatt's advice to hire a helper as my schedule quickly filled. I began Spanish lessons. I got involved on Sunday mornings in a local church and our family often went to a second church on Sunday evenings. I got involved in training Spanish women in Woman's Missionary Union work. I started my work in the seminary library. I spent time with my girls. And I also soon began to get an idea of just how many dinners I would be called on to prepare and host and how many overnight guests would enjoy our little guest room. A live-in helper would be a necessity – not a luxury – if I expected to do all I knew God wanted me to do.

❦

FINDING A CHURCH for our family was high on our to-do list. Because Bona Nova (Good News) Baptist Church was within walking distance of our apartment, it seemed logical that we visit there. The church quickly became our home church.

As we were preparing to attend our first Sunday service, Joyce Wyatt suggested I wear a small hat. I understood why when we got to the church and saw that all of the women had their heads covered with small *mantillas* (black veils). Joyce explained that most evangelicals in Spain believed Scripture teaches that women must cover their heads in church and most pastors taught that the covering was a sign of submission to their husbands. She and the other missionaries had been trying to teach them that "covering" had been specifically for New Testament days and wasn't necessary in 1957, but the practice remained. Many churches provided veils and some women carried extra veils in case some forgot theirs. In some church foyers, there was a cabinet with compartments for women to leave their veils and Bibles until the next time they came to church – I always wondered if they had other Bibles at home.

I must admit it was a beautiful sight to see so many women wearing their black veils. Yet, I knew I had a problem with what the veils represented. In time, I thought I had finally found a way to support the women who wore the veils and those of us who didn't. I decided to alternate between wearing a simple small hat or no head covering at all and wearing a *mantilla*. The first day I wore a *mantilla*, I caused quite a stir. Most of the women and some of the men kissed me on both cheeks. One young man ran down the street after church to kiss me and let me know how happy he was to see me wearing the veil.

One Sunday I was sitting in front of some elderly women – who all were covered, of course. I wasn't wearing my veil that day. Plus, it was my alternate day, so I didn't even have on a hat. One of the women reached in her bag and pulled out a thick and rather smelly heavy black veil and placed it on my head. I returned it to her graciously with thanks and told her it wasn't my Sunday to cover. I didn't turn around to gauge her and her friends' reactions, but they did remain friendly with me over the next weeks.

❧

ONE SUNDAY SOON after we had joined Bona Nova, I was standing at the back of the sanctuary talking with the pastor when suddenly a door to a Sunday school (Bible study) classroom flew open and a young woman came out crying. The pastor told me the class was a small group of young teenage boys and that he didn't know what he was going to do with them. He further said, "It happened again. Every week or so they do or say something to hurt their teacher's feelings. They think it's amusing. They show no respect for a teacher, and no one wants to teach them."

I immediately said, "Let me try." I was about to add "Sunday school teacher" to my growing list of responsibilities.

The pastor was shocked and said, "They will just hurt you the way they hurt her. I can't let you do that." I assured him that I had taught that age group in the States – in English, of course – but I felt confident I could do it with my beginning Spanish. Obviously, he didn't know what else to do with the class, so he finally agreed. He, however, wasn't very hopeful.

The next Sunday I came well prepared. I hoped I wouldn't make too many mistakes in the language. I'd thought of methods I'd used in the U.S. and had chosen some I thought would fit the lesson and would challenge the boys. I was surprised when I learned there was one girl in the class, along with five boys.

That first Sunday I told them I didn't speak their language well and wanted them to help me by not interrupting the class, unless I asked for help. They were respectful and agreed.

The first class went well, with no interruptions. We had contests, which kept them thinking about getting more right answers than the opposing team and not about creating distractions. Plus, that kept their minds off my language flaws. They responded respectfully when I asked questions, and no one laughed when I made a mistake in my limited Spanish. They were delighted to respond when I asked the proper pronunciation of a word or the preferred use of another.

Soon after I started teaching that class, promotion time – the time when students move up to the next age-level class – came. Our new class had more students, and we had to move to a larger room. I enjoyed the class immensely.

The lone girl who had been in the original class, Alicia – not her real name – was beautiful. Later, she and Linda became good friends. We learned that she had moved to Barcelona to work to help support her family who lived some distance away. She came to church with her aunt and the aunt's family, with whom she lived.

After some time, Alicia's parents wanted her to come home for a visit. That worried her aunt and her family – especially because Alicia had left the church of her parents, had accepted Christ as Savior, and had become a member of Bona Nova Baptist Church. Alicia and her aunt decided she should go home but that her cousin should accompany her to make sure she was allowed to return to Barcelona.

And so Alicia and her cousin made their way by bus to the remote village where Alicia's family lived. The bus didn't go all of the way to the village, so they had to walk the last miles.

Of course, Alicia's family was delighted to see her and her cousin. All went well until Sunday. That day, Alicia said she couldn't go to mass with her family. She told them she had come to know Christ personally and had become a member of a Baptist church. Her mother was enraged at the news, so much so that she took a butcher knife, held it to her breast, and said, "Go ahead. Kill me. That's what you are doing to me." Alicia began to cry. She didn't want to hurt her mother but neither could she deny her Savior.

Alicia's family insisted that she and her cousin go to mass, although for some reason the rest of the family didn't go. She and her cousin did go to the church that morning, but they didn't go inside. Instead, they stayed outside and cried.

That afternoon, Alicia's mother told her that her cousin would have to return to Barcelona alone – Alicia could not go with her. She would have to stay in the village and she would have to go to church with her family.

When the members of Bona Nova church heard about the situation, many of them began to pray for Alicia. Soon word came that Alicia was coming back to Barcelona to work because her family needed the money that she would send home. This time, however, an aunt was also going to come with her to see that she didn't return to the Baptist church.

About that time, Gerald and I began inviting my youth Sunday school class to our apartment on Sunday nights after church for food and fellowship. These teens loved to *pasear* – take a long walk together – after evening worship services, which served as a way to get to know each other without breaking into dates, something that wasn't done until there was a serious commitment or an engagement to marry. The youth loved the idea of walking to our apartment but said they didn't know the way, so Linda – who was about seven at the time – offered to lead them. They loved that, especially since Linda was already speaking Spanish as well as they did.

Our class increased our prayers for Alicia. We knew how much she wanted to be with us and how much she wanted to study the Bible. Then someone suggested that we invite her to our Sunday night fellowships and that we discuss the Bible lesson we'd studied that morning in Sunday school. It worked.

One Sunday morning as we were getting ready to pray for Alicia, to our amazement she walked in to Sunday school. She told us that she'd begged her aunt so much that finally she'd said she could come – but the aunt would have to come, too. Alicia said, "She's sitting over there in the back row by herself." After that day, they continued to come together. Before long the aunt said that Alicia had been right – she said it was good to worship God the way we did, and she made a profession of faith and joined Bona Nova Baptist Church.

❈

AS FOR LEARNING SPANISH, Gerald and I began our first Spanish lessons with Sr. Cuyas, Roy Wyatt's secretary, who had volunteered to teach us. I had one lesson with him and decided his method wasn't going to work for me – he'd made up a story about squirrels and was going to use that as the basis for his teaching. Plus, he wanted to teach us Spanish and Catalán – the language of the region of Catuluña – at the same time. That simply was too much. It took Gerald a little longer to decide Sr. Cuyas wasn't the teacher for him either. Eventually Gerald joined me to study with the teacher Joyce Wyatt had found. Her name was Sra. Torras.

Joyce had met Sra. Torras at the American Woman's Club, where she went in order to learn English. When Joyce had talked with her about teaching Gerald and me, Sra. Torras decided she would learn more English teaching two Americans who wanted to learn Spanish than by listening to speakers at the Woman's Club. Besides, she would get paid. A pharmacist, Sra. Torras was obviously intelligent. She even came to our apartment for our lessons, which was convenient because we didn't yet have a car and were just learning to use the subway system. For our first lessons, we used a book we had brought from the States.

Because I'd studied French for four years and because both French and Spanish are derived from Latin, I found it fairly easy to learn to read Spanish, but knowing French made it hard for me to learn to speak Spanish. At least that was my excuse for having to study so much.

Gerald had studied German at the Naval Academy and had continued with it at Georgetown College, which put him at a disadvantage in learning Spanish since it isn't a language derived from Latin. His German did prove beneficial as he could help our girls with their studies at the Swiss school where the principle language used was German.

While our studies with Sra. Torras set us on the right path, it was a lovely young university student who came to our apartment two or three times a week to read the Bible and pray with us who most helped us with the language. Esther Frances was the daughter of a pastor in the city of Valencia. She also spoke English very well.

Esther was a great teacher. We did have our funny moments, too. She often reminded us about when Gerald leaned to say *"Deuteronomio"* (Deuteronomy). He could make her laugh just by saying the word. As we got to know her, Esther told us that she hadn't been allowed to attend public school because she had no baptismal certificate from the Catholic Church. The fact that her father was a Baptist pastor also had played a big role in her not getting to go to public school. In spite of everything, her father had seen that she got an education. Each term, he had accompanied her to school to try to enroll her, but each term school officials hadn't let her enroll. They, however, had told him the names of the textbooks they would be using that year in her grade. And so each year, her pastor-father – who had little education himself – had taken it upon himself to teach her from those books. Thankfully, at the end of each term, she always had been allowed to take the final exam with the other students. Each time, she had scored *sobresaliente* (outstanding) and had been promoted to the next grade. In time, Esther became the first Spanish evangelical woman to graduate from a university.

Esther married Sr. Jose Borrás, a former Catholic priest who was a student at the Baptist seminary at the time they married. Because Jose had been a priest, he and Esther couldn't get married in Spain, so they went to England to marry. Later Sr. Borrás taught in the *Seminario Teológico Bautista* and then became Dean. Still later, he became director (president) of the seminary after Gerald had held that position for ten years.

Sr. Borrás' testimony of how he came to faith in Jesus has always inspired our family. He was well on his way to a career as a Catholic priest and was teaching in a school in Albacete. One day a nun in the school brought him a Bible that a student had turned in. Sr. Borrás immediately started tearing it up in front of his students – until he remembered that he was scheduled to give a lecture on the heresy of Protestantism and the threat Protestants posed. He decided to keep the Bible so he'd have more information with which to attack Protestantism. In the process of studying that mutilated Bible, he came to a life-altering decision. After much internal struggle and the alienation of many friends and family members, he came to declare "I have been studying the Bible, the Word of God, and I cannot continue as a Roman Catholic priest. I have to be true to my conscience. I have Jesus Christ in my heart and in my life, and He has pardoned me and given me eternal life."

Because of his decision, Sr. Borrás was stripped of all his extensive academic credentials and had to begin earning degrees – including his secondary school diploma – all over again. After he became a believer, he earned degrees from the European Baptist Theological Seminary in Rüschlikon, Switzerland; *Seminario Teológico Bautista* in Barcelona; and Union Theological Seminary in New York City.

Our daughters grew particularly fond of the Borrás family. Marsha was just two years old when Esther came to our home to speak Spanish with us. Esther tried to practice her English on Marsha, but our stubborn daughter would only speak to her in Spanish. Children can learn a language so easily and both Marsha and Linda were speaking Spanish well before their parents could speak it at all.

Many years later, it was Jose whom Marsha first told that she felt God was calling her to missions. At that time, she hoped to return to Spain. While Spain wasn't in God's plan for her, she has spent her life with her husband and sons serving in another area of the world.

❋

LEARNING A NEW language is a never-ending process, and both Gerald and I made our fair share of mistakes, especially during our first year. Thankfully, there was usually a kind national nearby who could translate for us and not laugh at our funny mistakes.

Missionaries, however, always remember those awkward and amusing moments. One morning as I was leaving home to go to work in the seminary library, I wanted to be sure that our helper mopped the kitchen floor, so I told Maria to mop *el techo*. She looked confused and asked *"el techo, Señora?"* I replied, *"Si, si, el techo."* I was asking her to mop the ceiling, even as I pointed to the floor. She didn't laugh then, but I bet she and the other maids in our building had a good laugh later.

For many locals, it was hard to understand our lack of conversational skills. One man said, *"No habla Español? Si aún mi nieto lo puede hablar!"* Translation: "She can't speak Spanish? Why, my four year old grandson can speak it!"

Mistakes in day-to-day conversation were embarrassing enough, but those made in church were even worse. One Sunday a teacher at church surprised me by asking me to pray. For the life of me, I simply couldn't remember how to start a prayer! The people didn't know I was silently asking God to help me out of that embarrassing moment. Thankfully, He answered my silent plea for help and I was able to voice a prayer.

I wasn't alone in making mistakes in our new language; Gerald made his share of mistakes, too. Spanish people are devoted to *fútbol* (soccer), so one year when the Barcelona team won the last game of a tournament Gerald went to his barbershop and casually said, "So the Barcelona team are the *champiñones* of Spain." He thought he was saying champions – *campeones* – but instead he was saying *champiñones* – mushrooms. He had said, "The Barcelona team are the mushrooms of Spain."

❧

AS SOON AS I could, I tackled the seminary library – which consisted of several empty stacks and fewer than fifty books, most of which were copies of current or past textbooks. After assessing the situation, I wrote to my sister-in-law Ida Hall, who was a high school librarian in Louisville, and asked her advice. She recommended a book on classification. I was ready to get to work. (Of course, all my work would be in Spanish.)

The typewriter in the library office was ancient but usable. Then a friend in Louisville whose husband was changing jobs wrote to ask if I could use an excellent typewriter. Could I!

I had worked in two college libraries but never in a theological library and so at my first opportunity, I went with Gerald to the European Baptist

Theological Seminary in Rüschlikon, Switzerland. I'd heard the seminary had an excellent library. The librarian there was very helpful.

When I returned from Switzerland, I asked for a budget for the library and got to work. I was always careful about the purchase of new books and almost always consulted with a professor before I bought one. By the time Gerald and I retired thirty-three years later, the library had more than 5,000 books as well as historical material about many of the Baptist churches in Spain.

I thoroughly enjoyed my library work. After all, it was one of the ministries to which God had called me. In addition to helping students with research, there were special moments with special people. The son of one of the students loved to find me in the library stacks and ask me, *"Señora, cuéntame un cuento."* Translation: "Señora, tell me a story." He loved my attention and never tired of asking me to share a story. That little boy was Julio Diaz, who is president of *Seminario Teológico Bautista* in 2015.

❀

SHORTLY AFTER WE arrived in Spain, Gerald was asked to serve on the national Sunday school committee of the Spanish Baptist Convention. Little did we know that assignment would continue for the next thirty-two years. For all those years, Gerald was often away from home from Thursday through Saturday, arranging for Sunday school teacher training events all over Spain. For ten of those years, he was also national Sunday school promoter. Initially, he was paired with a Spanish pastor who spoke English, which was a great help as Gerald learned Spanish. In later years, I also participated in the teacher training events, leading classes on how to teach children and other such topics.

Throughout our years in Spain, we always wanted Spanish Baptists to know how much we desired to work alongside them, so early on we invited a colleague from the national Sunday school committee and his wife to eat at our home. They were very gracious and both spoke English. I don't remember what I served, but I'm sure it was a typical American meal, complete with hot yeast rolls, which is one of my specialties. The table was beautiful, the children were in bed, and we adults sat down to enjoy our meal. Then I noticed our guests had each taken a roll and put it on the bread plate but the wife wasn't eating hers. I noticed that every time the husband reached for his roll, his wife would touch his hand and he would draw it back. I just couldn't understand since we knew Spaniards ate a lot of bread. What I didn't know was that they didn't eat hot bread. Later Gerald and I learned that hot bread was thought to be dangerous to one's health. We had a lot to learn!

❀

IN 1958, GERALD and I were given a wonderful opportunity to travel outside Spain. Because no other Baptist missionaries and no national pastor was available, we were asked to attend the European Baptist Federation meeting in Germany. We took seven-year-old Linda with us and left Marsha with the Hilliards. We knew that Marsha and the Hilliards' older daughter, Rose, played well together. Marsha was delighted with the arrangement.

We traveled by train since a trip by car would not only have been difficult but also expensive. We changed trains at the French border, and then we exchanged currency at the German border. When the train reached the corridor between East and West Germany and the official came around to collect our fare, we were surprised when he asked us for East German *marks,* which we didn't have. It seems the corridor was owned by East Germany and neither our West German *marks* nor our French *francs* would be accepted – something no one had told us before we left Spain. The official told us that we would have to leave the train at the next station. When other passengers heard that, they became alarmed. They knew that station was not a good one for foreigners – especially Americans, and especially at night. What were we going to do?

Thankfully, a British man said, "I'll pay their fare," which he did. He explained to us and all the gathered passengers that he had attended the Billy Graham crusade in London the previous year and because he was so grateful for Billy Graham, he would do anything for an American. He not only paid our fare but also gave me his seat. Linda sat on my lap until we arrived in West Berlin.

Throughout the journey, we saw evidences of World War II, which had ended thirteen years before. We saw many people – especially men – who had lost a limb, or even two. We saw bombed-out buildings standing as reminders of the horrors of war. When we arrived at our hotel in West Berlin, Linda was especially disturbed by the remains of a bombed-out church that we could see from our hotel window.

While we were in Germany, we ate lunch with a beautiful, intelligent German girl who had experienced the war first-hand and was living in East Germany. She told us that she had needed to secure special permission to attend the Baptist meeting in West Berlin that day and would have to cross the border back into East Germany before nightfall. As she told us about her life there, she expressed gratitude for America's part in ending the war.

The earth is the LORD's,
and everything in it,
the world, and all who live in it;
for he founded it upon the seas
and established it upon the waters.
Psalm 24:1-2

EIGHT

❀

Two years into our first term in Spain, the decision was made to close the seminary for the 1959-60 academic year since most of the missionaries who were on the faculty would be on furlough in the United States and only two Spanish part-time professors would be left. That opened the opportunity for Gerald, the girls, and me to experience a very different area of Spain than what we had seen in Barcelona and to address some specific ministry needs there.

We stored our small stash of personal furnishings in the seminary building, left our beautiful apartment on Calle Balmes, and moved 250 miles down the coast to Alicante. The pastor of Alicante Baptist Church knew of Gerald's experience in Sunday school work and wanted his help.

From the start, we loved the friendliness of the people in the Alicante church. Plus, right away, Linda and Marsha spotted a *pipas* (sunflower seeds) cart right outside the church door. They loved the raw, salted sunflower seeds. Ah, we thought, this was where some of the harvest of the acres and acres of beautiful Spanish sunflowers ended up! (Of course, much of the harvest became sunflower oil.) The *pipa* seller would make a cone out of newspaper and ladle the *pipas* for the girls and their church friends. All the children always had *céntimos* at the ready to pay him. Today, Linda tells me that many secrets were told and new friendships were made around that *pipa* cart.

❀

WE'D BEEN TOLD that finding a home in Alicante would be very easy because the city was a popular site for tourists from England and Central and Northern Europe. It wasn't quite that easy. Because we arrived in vacation season, most apartments had already been rented to the tourists. We finally found one – though it was on the busy main street, which was the hub for all the streetcar lines that spread all over the city.

When Patsy Hilliard had learned that we would be moving to Alicante for a year, she'd suggested that her helper, Angustia, go with us to help us get settled. I didn't think that was necessary, but Patsy insisted. Angustia was more than happy to go, happy to be taking what she called a *vacación* (vacation). I doubt that she'd been outside Barcelona before.

Angustia kept our girls amused on the long seven-hour trip over very bad roads to Alicante. In those days, often highways were repaved, rough Roman roads that didn't necessarily take a direct route. Along the way to Alicante, Angustia and the girls played *"cuenta los cementerios"* – "count the cemeteries" – on the sides of the road. About 500,000 people had lost their lives in the Spanish civil war, so there were many cemeteries across the country. In Spain, the cemeteries are very different from the typical cemetery in the States. The dead are buried in above-ground family vaults, with only four people in each vault. If a family member has recently been buried in a vault and then another family member dies, the family vault isn't opened immediately. Instead, the family borrows or rents a vault until the required time has elapsed; then the body is moved to the family vault. One time, Gerald and I attended a funeral where the body of the last person to be placed in the family vault was removed and set on the floor before us. The body was easily recognizable as someone we knew well. I won't write what came next, but I was glad that we hadn't brought the girls.

On the trip Angustia also entertained the girls with songs and stories. They continued to sing this one long after Angustia returned to her home with the Hilliards: *"Parece que va a llover, Los cielos se están nublando, Parece que va a llover. Ay, Mamá, me estoy mojando."* Translation: "It looks like it's going to rain. The sky is getting cloudy. It looks like it's going to rain. Oh, Mama, I'm getting wet."

When darkness fell, the road to Alicante became confusing, and we took a wrong turn. By that time everyone was getting hungry, so we found a restaurant that looked promising. Before our food arrived, two dogs came in and lay under our table, apparently to catch any spare crumbs.

We finally arrived in Alicante and had no trouble finding our apartment. Thankfully, we arrived before 10 p.m., so the front door was unlocked. Had we arrived after 10, the story would have been different. In every apartment building in Spain, at precisely 10 p.m. every night, the outer doors were closed and locked. If you arrived after 10, the protocol was to stand on the sidewalk and clap your hands. Then the night watchman would come to unlock the door. Of course, you then had to give him a tip.

Once we were inside the apartment building, we did face a problem: The small elevator had the dreaded *"No Funciona"* (out of order) sign on it. Because we were afraid to leave anything visible in the car, we all lost a few pounds that night as walked up and down eight flights of steps several times, carting our belongings. On the first trip, Gerald carried Marsha and a suitcase, and I took Linda's hand and a smaller suitcase. I'm afraid Gerald bore the brunt of those many trips.

❖

THE SETTING FOR OUR APARTMENT was lovely. The apartment building was on a wide street lined with palm trees on either side. We could see the Mediterranean Sea from both the dining room and bedroom windows. We told Marsha she would probably be a sailor because she loved to watch the ships on the Mediterranean so much. (Remember, too, how she'd loved to *drive* the ship on our voyage from New York to Barcelona.)

As for that elevator, it turned out frequently to have a *No Funciona* on the door – which wasn't a big surprise. A fellow missionary had told us that for a time after he first arrived in Spain he thought *"No Funciona"* were the Spanish words for elevator. Seven flights plus an additional mezzanine level meant a lot of steps for short little legs! (Some Spanish apartment buildings have an extra, unnumbered floor between the main floor and the first floor, which is the mezzanine.)

The apartment was furnished, albeit sparingly. The only seats were the chairs at the dining room table. The master bedroom had a bed and a closet. The girls' room had two twin beds and a nightstand with one very small drawer. The landlord had given us permission to bring a refrigerator and a wringer washing machine. When I asked to bring a chest of drawers, the landlady said, "Why? The drawer between the beds will hold all of the panties and socks your girls will have." (Because of her response, we didn't bring a chest of drawers.)

When we moved in, we noticed something that we hadn't seen when we'd walked through the apartment the first time: The kitchen range was not a range at all, but a two-burner hot plate sitting on a counter. As for the oven, there was no way to regulate the temperature, but at least it did have an on-and-off switch.

Another curious thing about the apartment was that the dining room and the kitchen were on the extreme opposite ends of the one central hall. I often said I needed roller skates to put food on the table. Since there was no room to eat in the kitchen, we ate all our meals in that dining room very far from the kitchen.

❁

LINDA WAS NOW in third grade. Home schooling was the only possibility in Alicante, so we quickly set up an area in the apartment to be our school. Gerald found some orange crates and stacked them to make a desk. Teaching Linda was one of the best experiences I've ever had. She was a good student and kept me on my toes. She always wanted to learn something new and was excited about everything she learned.

Linda already knew how to read German and Spanish, so I used our time to teach her to read English, which she seemed to swallow. Before I knew it, she was not only reading her school books and the supplemental material I'd brought but also the World Book Encyclopedia that we'd brought from the States. She enjoyed our lessons together, especially art history and Greek mythology. She kept up her German by studying with a neighbor once a week, and she and I read together the Spanish books that her classmates in the Swiss school were reading that year. (We had to continue to pay tuition to the Swiss School in order to reserve spots for both girls the next year.)

I didn't do one thing: I didn't insist that she write and do everything with her right hand as her teacher in the Swiss school would have done. Linda liked that. So did I.

Before Angustia returned to Barcelona, she found a young girl in our church to take Marsha for a long walk and play with her every afternoon. Anytime the girl was asked who Marsha was, she would respond, *"Una Americana."* Translation: "An American girl." Marsha, however, didn't agree and would always correct her by saying that she was an English girl because she spoke English. Of course, the girl and Marsha always spoke in Spanish.

Thinking Marsha would be bored while Linda and I were having school, Gerald and I arranged a little play space on our back balcony, perfect for a four-year-old. She loved it. We didn't put out anything she could climb on because our apartment was so high up in the sky. (I will write more about that Marsha and her balcony play space in chapter fourteen.)

In order to improve my Spanish accent, our pastor's daughter offered to come to the apartment and help me when I wasn't having school with Linda. Raquel's little girl played with Marsha while we worked. Raquel wouldn't accept money from us, but when we learned that she wanted a white pleated skirt – which was popular at the time – we gratefully gave her one.

❀

OUR HELPER IN Alicante didn't live with us. As was usual for a day helper, in addition to her salary she asked for a loaf of bread and three eggs to take home with her every day. She did the grocery shopping with money I provided, and she brought me the receipt and the change. One day soon after she came to work for us, I counted the change and noticed a small discrepancy. I didn't say anything because I knew anyone can make a mistake. However, the next time she shopped, the mistake was larger. That time I questioned her about it. She replied that she had kept some money for herself the first day and since I didn't say anything about it she had kept more the second time. Because I hadn't said anything, she thought I didn't care. I assured her that I did care. She continued to receive a normal salary and the extras we gave her. There were no more discrepancies.

Then I learned about the custom that shopkeepers all over Spain practiced of favoring a helper by giving her a receipt for more than the purchased items were worth. It seemed everyone knew about it and accepted it as the way to do things.

❁

GERALD, THE GIRLS, and I enjoyed living in Alicante. The city is set amid the lush orange crops of the Valencia region in the center of the *Costa Blanca* (White Coast) and has warm balmy weather. Alicante even has its own wonderful version of *paella,* Spain's national dish. The nearby pueblo of Gijona is known for its *turrón,* a nougat candy we especially enjoyed at Christmastime. Even today, Marsha and Linda love giving Gerald and me *turrón* for Christmas.

We loved walking on the beautiful *Esplanada* (walkway) that ran along the harbor and was composed of intricate mosaic tiles set in a wave pattern. The walkway was about 600 meters long and was lined with coconut palms. The harbor was used by small fishing boats outfitted with elaborate multi-globed lamps used for night fishing. We enjoyed watching the fishermen and their wives who sat on the pier each day and mended their nets. In 2015, both Linda and Marsha remember how watching those men and women made it easy to imagine the New Testament stories of fishermen mending their nets by the Sea of Galilee.

As happens with children who grow up speaking more than one language, Marsha often mixed her languages. One day as we were walking on the *Esplanada* after church, Marsha declared with alarm, "Papá! I left your *Biblia* green that said *tu nombre!*" Translation: "Daddy! I left your green Bible that has your name inside."

In Alicante, we enjoyed experiences that were different from anything we'd known before. For example, each morning we'd watch for the donkey cart with the man who brought our milk. He would park his cart in front of our building and bring a large aluminum container of milk up our eight flights of stairs. Then he would measure out a *litro* or whatever amount we wanted that day into a large bowl, which I held for him. We loved watching him as he adeptly poured the right amount of milk from his milk can – without using any measuring device. We then took the milk into our kitchen where we strained it to remove any foreign matter and poured it into our pasteurizer. We then put the pasteurizer on the stove and brought the milk to a boil. And finally, we put the milk in the refrigerator to cool. This was how we got fresh milk for at least the first ten years we lived in Spain.

We especially enjoyed our one Christmas in Alicante and will never forget how Gerald's imagination saved the day. We wanted a Christmas tree, but no one there had ever seen one and couldn't believe we really wanted to put a tree in our apartment. Gerald found a nursery with lovely trees but the owner wasn't about to cut down a tree for such a use. Gerald kept looking around the nursery and finally found a small tree that we could use if it just had a few more branches. The owner had been trimming trees and suggested Gerald take some branches from those he had cut off. So, mission accomplished. We had a tree made by God and Gerald. We added some ornaments and lights, and the girls were thrilled with it. Needless to say, all the locals who saw it were amazed to see a tree in the house.

I, too, had to engage my imagination in order to add to the Christmas festivities. Because of our oven, I knew I would have to put my life-long love for baking and elaborate cake decorating on hold until we moved back to Barcelona. (When I was growing up in Kentucky, it seemed like I was always decorating a cake or learning techniques from both my parents. They were quite a pair when they were working on a cake. Dad would always decorate his cakes lavishly, but Mother would use more elegant restraint.) There would be no elaborate baking for me in Alicante.

Looking back, when I think about that hot plate/stove and oven I'm surprised that I had the nerve to have company at all, much less bake a fruitcake. But I did, and one of our guests –fellow missionary Joyce Wyatt – declared it the best fruitcake she'd ever eaten. Granted, she was a gracious person, but I was glad that at the very last minute before baking the cake I'd looked at the batter again and gone to the refrigerator for inspiration. I found in it a jar of blackberry jam. I added the whole jar to the batter and it looked better. Indeed, a great imagination is good to have on the mission field.

That Christmas in Alicante, except for the fruitcake, stovetop chocolate oatmeal cookies had to do. I admit they really came in handy with all the company we had during that Christmas season.

That Christmas, we also set up a display on a long table in the living room. Marsha loved telling visitors about it. She would explain, in Spanish of course, "Here is a Bible. It tells the world (showing our globe) the story of Jesus (showing the manger scene), who was born in a stable. It tells us that Jesus is the light (showing a lit candle) of the world."

While our Spanish friends enjoyed seeing the tree in our apartment, we, in turn, loved their traditions. Spanish Baptists always met in church on December 25 to celebrate the birth of Jesus. That was followed by a day of Christmas fun on the 26th – the day of St. Stephen – when church members got together to celebrate with music, drama, poetry recitals, and refreshments. Dec. 26 was a real family celebration and a wonderful time to invite guests to church. On January 06 –*Reyes* (Epiphany) – our Spanish friends celebrated the arrival of the three kings. The night before, children put their shoes on the balconies of their apartments and filled them with straw for the camels. By the next morning, the straw had been replaced with gifts.

❀

OF COURSE, we'd moved to Alicante to help the church, so we began our work immediately. We learned that the current church building was new and much larger than the one the congregation had previously used – they had outgrown that one. Even though there could be no sign on the outside of the building to indicate the building was a church, somehow people found out, and more and more people began attending.

In one Sunday service, as the pastor was welcoming new people, a woman named Sra. Gertrudis was sitting beside me. She turned to me and said, *"Yo quiero ser la que espera afuera."* Translation: "I want to be the one who stands outside." I had no idea why she would say such a thing. After the service was over, I asked her what she'd meant.

What she said touched me greatly. "A neighbor invited me to church and I enjoyed it very much, but it had started to rain and when I glanced outside I saw my friend standing under an umbrella, looking through the window. At that time, the church building was so small that everyone couldn't fit inside. It touched me that my neighbor, who had invited me to church with her, had to stand outside in the rain so I would have a place inside." Now Sra. Gertrudis wanted to be the one *que espera afuera* so others could be inside. She wanted her church to grow.

Indeed, the congregation had continued to grow and soon needed an even larger building. But before they could move, the government had closed the church and a seal/lock had been placed on the door. That, however, wasn't the end of the story.

About that time, the United States was considering opening an air base in Spain and the Spanish government wanted the base very much. When President Harry Truman heard about the closing of the Baptist church in Alicante, he told the Spanish government that Spain could have the air base if the government would allow the church to be re-opened. The government complied. How we wished that President Truman had known about the many other churches that had been closed by the government, too!

❧

GERALD AND I had come to the Alicante church because we'd heard the church especially needed help with its Sunday school/Bible teaching program. I soon understood why. On our first Sunday there, after attending worship and checking on the girls in the nursery, I went to the sanctuary to look for the pastor's wife so we could go to Sunday school together. (Spanish churches usually had Sunday school after the morning worship service.) When I told her I wanted to go to Sunday school, she asked, "Why?" It seemed that Sunday school held very little attraction to adult church members and especially to women.

When I went to the small room where the adult Sunday school class met, I saw several men and only two elderly women sitting on the back row. I joined them there. One of the women was small but full of energy. Each time she wanted to answer a question, she would raise her hand and often jump up and down. The teacher wouldn't let her answer, even if none of the men knew the answer. In that case, the teacher would answer the question himself. I knew then what my work would be that year.

That morning I suggested to the pastor that the church start a Sunday school class for women. The pastor assured me that no one would come. Besides, he said he didn't have time to teach it. I offered to be the teacher and told him that even if only two or three women came, it would be worth it. Reluctantly, he agreed and announced that a new class for women would meet in the sanctuary the next Sunday. The pastor again warned me that I shouldn't be disappointed if no one came.

They did come. In fact, that next Sunday twenty-six women showed up, all bringing their Bibles. They were delighted to have a class of their own. That day the lesson was more like a devotional with comments from some of the women about how glad they were to have something to do in church besides cooking and cleaning for special occasions.

The women continued to attend. Little by little most of them lost their shyness and entered into discussions. Because Gerald and I would be in the church for only a few more months, I knew I needed to decide who could teach the class after we left. I soon realized that the person who seemed to have the most respect from the other women and seemed most interested in Bible study was Sra. Gertrudis – the woman who had wanted to stand outside in the rain.

One weekend our family had to go to Barcelona and I wasn't sure what to do about the women's class while I was gone. In class, I turned to Sra. Gertrudis and asked her if she would teach for me. She sadly said, "I wish I could do it, but I can't read." I had prayed for a teacher and she was the only one who had come to my mind. Now I really didn't know what to do.

A little later in the class time she said, "My daughter can read. She can read the lesson to me, and I can teach it to the others." I could tell she really wanted to teach and so I agreed. I told Sra. Gertrudis that I would pray for her.

When we returned to Alicante, I asked several women how the lesson had gone. They were full of praise for their substitute teacher. Later, Sra. Gertrudis told me about how she had studied the lesson. Each day that week, her daughter had read the lesson to her twice. Then Sra. Gertrudis had knelt beside her bed with her Bible and Sunday school study book open before her and prayed. I understood why she'd done such a good job.

Over the next months, Sra. Gertrudis was one of my most engaged class members. When it was time for our family to leave Alicante and move back to Barcelona, I asked Sra. Gertrudis if she would take my place. She agreed and also said she was learning to read. Naturally, I was delighted. Several years later, I learned she was still teaching and that she would occasionally ask another woman to teach, just as I had asked her to teach for me. I was reminded that I'd mentored her much as Miss Jo Platt had mentored me so many years before when I'd helped her with those eight-year-olds at Stanford Baptist Church in Kentucky.

❋

MEMORIES OF ALICANTE lived on into our family's future. Some years later Lila Mefford, our missionary colleague, was visiting the Alicante church on the way to Madrid where Gerald and I were living. That day a woman asked to be remembered to me and said, "Give greetings from me to Sra. June because she loved me." Lila replied, "You mean you love her, don't you?" The woman answered, "I do love her, but I know she loves me." When Lila shared the woman's greeting, I immediately remembered her. She was a very small woman who lived in a cave. I was glad to know she realized that I loved her and that she still remembered me and loved me, even after several years.

Years later as Linda was planning her wedding to Russell Hoffman in Louisville, she wished for a wedding *mantilla* from Alicante, which was known for skilled lace making. She didn't know that her dad and I would make a special trip there to buy the *mantilla* she wore as a veil in her wedding.

❋

WE'D ONLY BEEN IN ALICANTE a short time when a committee from Elche Baptist Church visited us and asked Gerald to become interim pastor. Elche is a beautiful town known for the *Palmerál de Elche*, a magnificent palm grove dating back ten centuries to the time of the Moors. The largest palm grove in Europe, it has more than 200,000 palms of many varieties.

The Elche church wanted Gerald to come as interim pastor for a very specific reason: They wanted to continue holding services in their church building that had been closed by government order and had been sealed with a seal/lock on the front outside door. They explained that their pastor was suffering from a heart ailment and felt he needed to resign and move nearer his family. They told us that even though the church was officially closed, they could still hold services in the upstairs apartment where their pastor had lived because by law the government couldn't close the entrance to a private dwelling. (Most Spanish Baptist pastors lived in apartments above their churches.)

It seemed that in the Elche church, a second outside door led to a narrow stairwell that went to the upstairs apartment and that door could not be sealed. Once inside that second door, an interior door led to the sanctuary, which had been sealed. (Linda remembers well the eye-level crack in the door jamb next to the seal. When she looked through the crack, she could see beams of daylight – indicating that the ceiling was missing – and a large piece of dusty demolition equipment.)

As we heard more of the story of the Elche church, our hearts ached. When the authorities had come to place the seals/locks on the doors, the pastor had been very courageous and said, *"Bueno, pues cierren la iglesia, pero primero van a tener que matarme."* Translation: "All right, close the church, but you'll have to kill me first." The officials had simply removed him and continued with their work. The government then sent bulldozers to compromise the structure of the sanctuary and make it impossible to use. That's why the ceiling was missing.

❀

EVEN THOUGH WE'D moved to Alicante to give much-needed help to that church, the need in Elche seemed to us to be more urgent. Because the two towns were only about twenty minutes apart, we decided we could continue to live in Alicante and help the Elche church as well. Gerald could attend the morning service and Sunday school in Alicante and then go to Elche to preach in the evening service. Given that most Spanish churches had – and still have – their main service on Sunday evening, we knew that would work well. The girls and I planned to accompany him to the Elche church.

Remember, this was only our third year in Spain. For Gerald, it was intense. He continued to study Spanish with a tutor. He helped both the Alicante and the Elche churches. He preached almost every Sunday – which meant preparing and delivering sermons in Spanish. He traveled to churches to help with Sunday school teacher training, leaving home on Thursday and returning late Saturday in time to be in Alicante and Elche on Sunday. And in his spare time, he worked on writing the lectures in Spanish in New Testament and Biblical Archaeology that he would give when we returned to the seminary in Barcelona in the fall.

❖

VERY QUICKLY attendance began to grow at the Elche church, and we soon packed the meeting room in the apartment. Gerald said that sometimes he had to hold his Bible high because if he didn't, there would be a head underneath it. The stairway to the apartment provided extra seating and was often filled with church members. Even if they couldn't see the preacher, they could at least hear him. More than once Linda sat on my lap and Marsha sat on hers. And next to us, Linda's best friend, Aurora, sat on her mother's lap with Marsha's friend, Esther, on Aurora's. It wasn't long before we all loved going to the Elche church.

Sometimes we'd receive advance warning that the police were planning to come by to check to see how many people were attending a worship service in a closed church. For the safety of the members, at those times we'd move the service to the home of a church member. In those homes, sometimes we'd worship in a back enclosed patio and at other times in the largest room in the house. If the largest room were a bedroom, the church deacons would dismantle and pull out the furnishings and put in chairs. After the worship service, they would stack the chairs and put the furniture back in place. The nomadic existence of our congregation was sometimes tiring but it never was discouraging to the people. In fact, the congregation continued to grow and thrive.

Whenever the authorities chased us out of one home, we would go to another. In reality, the authorities tried to discourage us from meeting anywhere at all – but their strategy didn't work. Something kept drawing the people back to the pastor's apartment in the closed church building. Actually, the authorities probably liked that meeting place best because they could keep an eye on us there. When someone asked one church member how long the people could keep it up, the man said, *"Algun dia van a tener que rendir, porque nosotros nunca nos vamos a rendir."* Translation: "Someday they will give up and stop chasing us, but we'll never give up."

For Gerald and me, at first the idea of defying the police required some thought and prayer. We'd been taught to obey the law in everything and now we were deliberately doing the opposite. Seeing the seriousness of evangelicals in Spain helped us to grasp their reasoning. Their obvious devotion to the Lord and His church helped us understand their willingness to defy the authorities. The Lord put love for the Spanish Christians in both of us so that it was painful to see them hurt when we knew what they'd been through as individuals and as churches.

Finally, the governmental authorities gave up on checking up on our church. Because attendance was growing instead of diminishing, they decided we could resume using the sanctuary. In the process of reopening the space, it was discovered that the stairway was unsafe because the supports had been removed. The authorities advised that only one person could be on the stairway at a time. Can you imagine? That was the stairway that had often been filled to overflowing with worshipers listening to Gerald's sermon. Then, the room at the top of the stairs – which had become our substitute sanctuary – was inspected. And when the officials looked into the room where children had met and mothers had tended to their babies during worship, they wouldn't even enter it. They said that no one should ever go in it again. As with the stairs, there were no supports underneath it. We soon realized that those government bulldozers that had set out to compromise the integrity of the building had destroyed nearly all the support of what was left of the building. Who, we asked ourselves, had held that room up while mothers quieted their babies and while young girls had their meetings before church? We realized we'd been part of a miracle.

Our family had many wonderful experiences at Elche Baptist Church. The New Year's Eve service was an especially happy one. First, we enjoyed refreshments and singing and then as midnight approached, everyone gathered in a circle, held hands, and prayed the New Year in. To this day, our girls remember that night as the simplest, most beautiful New Year's Eve experience of their lives.

❁

ONE SUNDAY, in addition to attending morning services at Alicante and preaching in the evening service at Elche, Gerald also preached at a mission/satellite church in a nearby village. That day, the church celebrated his coming with a *paella*. It had been cooked over a wood fire and was served in the typical and preferred way in a giant, round *paella* pan.

When everyone sat down to eat, Gerald noticed there was a fork but no plate at each person's place. He soon learned why: Everyone ate from the big pan in which the *paella* had been prepared. Gerald proceeded to carefully build walls around the food directly in front of him and then ate from that – he was surely the only one doing so. When one of the hostesses thought he wasn't getting enough to eat, she grabbed his fork from his hand and began to put more food in front of him, tearing through his carefully constructed walls. Later, he did admit that he'd gotten some very choice portions.

Early on, I'd learned that when *paella* is served, often a special treat is given to the guest of honor: *La cabeza del conejo* – a rabbit's head. The entire head is cooked in the *paella* pan and then is placed in an upright position on the guest of honor's plate of *paella*. (I don't think Gerald got a rabbit's head that day.) The first time I was served the rabbit's head I was also asked to pray. I have no idea what I prayed as I stared down at those beady eyes!

❁

FOR ALL OF THE THIRTY-THREE YEARS we served in Spain, letters were the only economical way to communicate with family and friends back in the States. And those letters took at least ten days to cross the Atlantic. Occasionally telegrams were used in the case of a death. Even as late as 1974, Linda sent us a telegram with the words "all ok" after a devastating tornado had hit Louisville. And in 1980, she announced the birth of her son, Matthew, by telegram.

Not long after we'd moved to Alicante I received a letter from my sister Edna saying that our mother was in the hospital. Edna wrote me that Mother had breast cancer and was scheduled for surgery the next day. I knew that by the time I had received the letter, Mother's surgery would have been over.

That day I wanted desperately to talk with someone who could pray with me. Gerald was out of town. We hadn't been in Alicante very long so I knew no one except the pastor and his family. Our girls were with me, but they were four-and eight-year olds. Plus, we didn't have a telephone or a car. So there was no one.

As I prepared for bed that night, I opened my Bible to try to gain some comfort. I don't remember what passage I read, but it didn't really matter because I was so physically and mentally tired that I hardly knew what I was reading. I didn't even know how to pray for my mother, who was so far away. Edna had written that when the doctors had told the family about the cancer, Daddy had cried but Mother hadn't. I knew Mother's faith was so strong and beautiful that she could sincerely say, "Thy will be done," and then relax.

I tried to pray like that, but I felt so far away from my family that it seemed impossible. I finally gave up and went to bed. I must have gone to sleep because when I woke up I remembered having had a beautiful dream. I'd dreamed I was kneeling by my bed and praying. As I looked toward the door, I saw a beautiful sight. There stood a figure dressed entirely in white. I wasn't afraid or even surprised when I saw the figure. Then the figure said, "She's going to be alright," and slowly disappeared. After I work up from the dream, I went back to sleep and slept until morning.

To this day I can't explain how I felt that morning. I do know that was one of the most touching experiences I have ever had.

We waited six weeks before we received another letter. Mother had had her surgery, and her doctor said she would be fine – just as the figure in my dream had said.

Many times over the next years we would experience how difficult it is to deal with family tragedies and deaths from such a distance. When my sister Mary Catherine's son Byron died, we learned the news by letter. When Gerald's father died, we were traveling in Portugal and learned of his death from missionaries there, who had been notified by our Board. They told us when we arrived; Gerald's father's funeral had been held several days before. We learned about Gerald's mother's death by telephone. When my father died, we also learned by telephone. We knew when we went to Spain that it wouldn't be possible to return to the States when family members died, so we expected this. Still, it was hard. And my mother?

Even though she was ill, she promised that she would stay alive until Gerald and I retired. And she did!

❀

AFTER OUR YEAR in Alicante and Elche, we returned to Barcelona for Gerald to resume teaching seminary classes with a new group of students and for me to resume my work in the seminary library. I added teaching English, New Testament, and Old Testament to student wives to my list of ministry responsibilities. Linda began fourth grade at the Swiss School and Marsha started half-day kindergarten.

We found a furnished apartment on Calle Via Augusta almost directly across the street from the Swiss School. Calle Via Augusta was on the same subway line we'd used before, so we knew all the stops. That was especially advantageous for me because I have a poor sense of direction.

As for the apartment, we were surprised by the décor. In the living room, the sofa and two comfortable chairs were upholstered in bright orange and black. Even the backs of the furniture were black. One visitor from the U.S. looked into our living room and said, "Wow, this has personality." I replied, "Yes, but it's unfortunately *not* my personality."

One bedroom had two twin-sized beds. Another room had one-twin sized bed and was the smaller of the two rooms and had a little balcony off of it. Marsha claimed that one for herself, since she had never had her own room. We agreed that it could be hers on the condition that she would sleep in Linda's room when we had overnight guests.

During those days, Señor Fontanet, who was pastor of a church in Lerida two hours away, often stayed with us and came to our house late at night because of the train schedule. On those nights, Gerald would carry Marsha from her room to Linda's room. Any time Marsha woke up in Linda's room, she would ask, *"Está aqui Señor Fontanet?"* Translation: "Is Señor Fontanet here?"

Many guests came and went. Some were missionaries and others, like Sr. Fontanet, were Spanish nationals. Some were American Christians who had come to work alongside us.

❀

GERALD AND I had gone to Spain to share the Gospel and opportunities to talk about our faith in Jesus came in many unexpected ways. One day a gypsy woman came to our door offering tablecloths, which wasn't unusual as people selling their wares often appeared at our door. What was unusual was that while I usually said, *"No gracias,"* that time I said, "I'll buy your tablecloth if you will let me give you something and tell you about it."

We always kept a supply of evangelistic tracts on a table near the door, but that day I reached for a New Testament instead. When the woman saw it, she began to cry. She told me her daughter had recently become a Christian and had written asking her mother to send her a Bible. She said, "That's why I'm selling tablecloths today. I want to buy her a Bible." I asked if she understood her daughter's decision to become a Christian. She said she didn't but was willing to let me tell her how she, too, could have an experience like that of her daughter.

I thought that she, too, needed a Bible, so I told her I would give her a Bible for her daughter if she would let me give her one, too. And I asked her if I could read a little from the Bible right then and there. As I read, tears ran down her cheeks. She didn't make a commitment that day – and I never saw her again – but even in 2015 I sometimes think of her and pray for her and her daughter. And the tablecloth is still in our family.

❁

IN MANY WAYS, our first term of service set the pace and tone for our thirty-three years in Spain. Looking back, so much of our long-term ministry began during those first four years. In those four short years, God had provided so many opportunities, and it seemed that many came at the same time. All those opportunities opened doors to more blessings than we could have ever imagined, especially in an ever-growing appreciation for God's workers among the Spanish people. What a delight and honor to work alongside them!

MOTHER AND DAUGHTER Nancy Hall proudly shows
off her first born, Beverly June Hall.1924

NEWLY WED June Hall McNeely. 1947

NAVAL MIDSHIPMAN Gerald McNeely, U.S. Naval Academy, Annapolis, Md. 1945

FIRST SUNDAY IN SPAIN Gerald and June McNeely and daughters Linda (standing) and Marsha attend their first Sunday worship service in Spain. 1957

TEACHING June McNeely leads a class for Spanish Baptists in how to teach children. 1962

OFF TO COLLEGE Sisters Linda McNeely (right) and Marsha McNeely wait at the Barcelona, Spain, airport for the flight that will take Linda to the States to begin college. 1969

TRAINING LEADERS Gerald and June McNeely prepare to lead a Sunday school training session at a church in Spain. 1982

SEMINARIO TEOLOGICO BAUTISTA. This building, which houses the Baptist Theological Seminary, was constructed during the time Gerald McNeely served as seminary president.

THANKSGIVING Gerald and June McNeely, at age 89, enjoy Thanksgiving Day in Louisville, Kentucky. 2013

Your attitude should be the same as that of Christ.
Philippians 2:5

NINE

That first term, Gerald and I were blessed more than we could ever have imagined. The pace was fast, but the certainty of being where God had called us kept us focused and humbled. There was much work to be done. We were amazed that the God who had called us to serve three wonderful congregations in the United States had sent us to such a beautiful country in which to live and work. Each place we had served seemed to add to the other and yet each was distinctly a part of His continuing call for us.

We were where God wanted us to be and there was so much to do. From the very beginning, we found our lives revolving far more around our Spanish colleagues than our American ones. The Spanish students were eager to learn to fulfill their own calls to share the love of Christ into the far corners of Spain and we wanted to help them. Pastors and church members were happy to work with us. And, as had happened in our churches in the States, we were developing deep friendships that would last for decades.

Gerald certainly had his hands full. He had gone to Spain in response to a request for a New Testament teacher in the seminary. Suddenly, he was told he would also be expected to teach Biblical Archeology in his second year in Spain. While he had taken one course in biblical archeology at Southern Seminary when he was working on his master of divinity degree, he had barely gotten his foot in the water. And so, in addition to his language studies – after all, he would be teaching all his classes in Spanish – he studied long and hard for this additional assignment. Often he felt overwhelmed, but he knew that with God's help, he could do it. And he did.

Gerald also wanted to help begin churches, so he was thrilled when Don Felix Fontanet – for whom Marsha often gave up her bedroom – asked him about beginning a new church in Zaragoza, about 180 miles west of Barcelona and about ninety miles from Lerida where Felix lived and was pastor of the Baptist church there.

The story of how a young Felix had become a believer in Jesus had been inspiring to us, as were the stories of many Spanish Baptists whom we came to know and love over the years. Felix had grown up in a small village that didn't have an evangelical church. One morning, some members of the Baptist church in a village several miles away visited his village and left evangelical literature and Bibles on the doorsteps of several homes. When one of Felix' neighbors found the material on his doorstep, he took it to Felix and said, "I can't read, but I know you can. I want you to have it."

Felix loved to read, and so he began to read the mysterious book his neighbor had given him. It was the Bible. When he heard about a church in a town five miles away, he wanted to go there and learn more, but he didn't have a car and there was no public transportation to the town. No problem: Felix walked the five miles to that church to find someone who believed the Bible.

Soon Felix became a believer. By the time Gerald and I arrived in Spain in 1957, he had attended seminary and was pastor of the Baptist church in Lerida. And now the Lord had burdened him for Zaragoza, the third largest city in Spain, which had only one evangelical church.

During the summer when seminary wasn't in session, Gerald and Felix began visiting in Zaragoza. On Mondays, Gerald drove to Lerida, picked up Felix, and together they went to Zaragoza and stayed until Thursday morning. Their church-planting method was to pass out evangelical tracts in apartment buildings, starting with the top floor and working their way down. Some people even invited them in to lead Bible studies.

Since there was no money to fund what they were doing, they often slept on pews in the evangelical church. They even found some old bedsprings to use. They hoped to find some mattresses but that never materialized, so after longs days of visitation, they slept on those hard springs.

Then somehow a local priest found out where they were staying and spread the word around. One night when they got back to the church, they saw that rocks had been thrown through several windows, resulting in broken glass strewn over the floor and pews.

Eventually, they did locate an elderly couple who'd been members of First Baptist Church in Madrid, and the couple invited them to sleep in their home. The bedroom where Gerald and Felix slept was the size of a small closet, and the bed was small for six-feet-two Felix and Gerald – but it had a mattress! The Espi's home was very humble and the meals were meager, but there was plenty of love.

Finally, Gerald and Felix got permission to use a spare room in a non-evangelical church for services. In order to make the space look more church-like, they needed chairs, a pulpit, and a curtain to pull across the front of the room to cover a window. Gerald and I gave the money we'd been saving to buy new curtains to replace some in our house that were too small, and we also donated a portable organ that the Woman's Missionary Union group in our church back in Carlisle, Kentucky, had sent us.

(When time came for our first furlough and our family left for furlough in the States, Don Felix and missionary Russell Hilliard continued to visit in the community and hold services in that room. Almost thirty-two years later as we prepared to leave Spain for retirement, we visited the church. By then, the congregation was meeting in a beautiful building on the opposite side of town and was talking about using that old room as a place to begin another new church. We were honored to have been part of the birthing of that church and were delighted to see the church's fervor to birth a new one.)

❁

NOT LONG INTO OUR FIRST TERM, we learned just how many dinner guests and house guests we would be entertaining over the years. Fortunately, I'd always loved entertaining and Gerald and I both loved the intellectual companionship of like-minded people as well as having our girls exposed to so many people from so many backgrounds.

From the beginning of our years in Spain, we regularly had dinner guests three or four nights a week. We also had frequent over-night guests, some of whom were last minute arrivals. To be sure, that was typical for missionary families because limited money made staying in hotels too costly. When we traveled to meetings in other parts of Spain and across Europe, we, too, were the beneficiaries of missionary hospitality.

Feeding so many people meant many hours shopping for groceries, especially after we returned to Spain from our first state-side furlough and no longer employed a live-in helper and I began doing all the grocery shopping myself. I will admit that shopping for groceries in Spain was delightful – if you had the time to spend. Produce was local and fresh and the selection was plentiful, though seasonal. Of course, you couldn't buy bread in the same shop where you bought eggs. Condiments were in yet another shop, buying meat required a trip to the meat market, and buying fish required a trip to the fish market, etc. Plus, often the markets weren't located anywhere near each other.

The first actual supermarket in Spain was a display model sent from the U.S., which was used for training employees and introducing shoppers to the supermarket concept. The food from that demonstration supermarket was donated to orphanages and nursing homes. The first supermarket that opened to the public had a first-floor garage with elevators to the upper floors. The food displays were all artistically arranged, as that is the nature of the Spanish people.

One day I watched as a well-dressed woman entered a new market and eyed a row of wheeled grocery carts. She asked a clerk to get one for her. She then started walking through the store, telling the clerk what to put in the cart. Even with new conveniences, some traditions remained the same. That day I'd run into the supermarket in a rush to buy eggs because unexpected company was coming and I found that I'd also run into an age-old custom as well. I watched as the clerk carefully individually wrapped each of my eggs in newspaper. She then bundled them into a little package and tied it with string. As I left, I saw the woman with the shopping cart – still walking around the market telling the clerk what she wanted him to put in her cart.

Preparing a meal was also labor-intensive. I always soaked lettuce and other produce that grew near the ground in *lejía* (bleach). I always made sure to have our cloth bread sack washed, dried, and ironed to be ready when I went to market. Because bread only came in baguette form and with no wrapping, there was no way to keep it separate from the other grocery items. Every woman in the market had her own cloth bread sack. Many years later, a bread truck came to our apartment building each day, and our *portero* (doorman) kept our bread order on a table in the entry to the building until we could retrieve it.

Washing the dishes for so many guests also presented challenges. When we entertained our Spanish friends, we served the food in courses, Spanish-style. There was a soup course, a salad course, and an entrée. Lots of dishes to wash! In both our apartments in Barcelona, the water from the hot water heater was never very warm, so I heated water in two big pans on the stove to wash dishes.

Of course, having so many over-night guests meant laundry day was intense, especially with using a wringer washer. I had to heat the water in pans on the kitchen stove, fill the washer tub, and set to work. Many times, I washed six sets of bed linens, plus six sets of towels and hung them to dry on those clotheslines that stretched between apartments. I knew that we would have more guests that night and I that I needed to get the beds ready. One day, in my hurry, I ran my fingers into the wringers. That injury led to arthritis, which I've had to deal with from that day until this.

I had to think constantly about the electrical situation. The electricity was not reliable and was often tripped by someone living in the building. However, after we bought a clothes dryer another issue was of my own making: If I forgot and had the hot water heater on or used the iron or used anything that required electrical current while I was running the dryer, then the circuit breaker would trip in the apartment below us. And it wasn't just the dryer that could cause a problem. One time when I tried to iron while the electric oven was on, I blew out all the lights in the entire apartment building. (Problems with electricity didn't just happen at home. Once as Gerald and I were showing slides to two different groups in two separate rooms in a church, the power went off. We'd blown a fuse on the street and the entire block had lost electric power.)

When I did use the dryer, I sat at the table and graded papers, wrote letters, and planned lessons. Looking back, at least that forced me to sit down for a while. Like Mother, I wasn't ever one to waste time.

As for heat in our first apartments, a coal furnace in the kitchen and a fireplace in the living room were our only sources. We ordered our coal from a man who came to our door and delivered our purchase to our coal bin in the basement. Gerald brought the coal up to our apartment and shoveled it into the stove. Since the fire would die down overnight, the apartment was very cold in the early mornings. When the girls got out of bed, they would run down the cold, tile hall and dress in front of the fireplace in the living room. Eventually, those buildings got central heating, which was rationed by the *portero* (doorman). Even as late as 1975, heat was still rationed, and we had hot water only about four hours a day.

❀

GERALD, THE GIRLS, and I enjoyed our guests immensely. We hosted Americans, fellow missionaries who lived in other parts of Spain who came to Barcelona for meetings, fellow missionaries from across Europe, and Spanish Baptists.

One guest especially delighted us. Virginia Wingo was a Southern Baptist missionary in Italy whom I'd first met at the Woman's Missionary Union Training School in Louisville. When we heard that Virginia and two missionary families from Italy were going to visit Spain, we planned to invite them to our home for a meal. Because it was summer and few students would be on campus, we assumed they would be staying at the seminary. That, however, was not to be.

One night as I was getting the girls ready for bed, I answered the phone to hear, "June, this is Virginia Wingo. You or Gerald come down to the train station to get me. Everyone is staring at me." It seems that when she and the other missionaries had arrived at the Spanish border, one of the women had discovered that she'd left her passport in Italy – who knows how she had gotten into France from Italy. Instead of returning to Italy with the group, Virginia had decided to come on to Barcelona and, I suppose, assumed someone would be available to meet her.

Gerald rushed to the train station and I stayed home to make up a bed. At nearly six feet tall, it was no wonder that everyone was staring at Virginia. (That reminds me that Marsha once said "Mommy, you are so short in America, but in Spain you are a giant." A giant at five feet tall?)

Virginia had brought her Italian espresso coffeemaker and coffee with her and constantly brewed espresso during her stay with us. At the time, we were packing for our move to Alicante, which led Gerald to tell her, "Virginia, I fully expect to open a trunk in Alicante and have you jump out with a cup of coffee." Our poor helper, Ana, was too polite to refuse Virginia's constant offers of coffee or even to put milk in it, so she became the most frequent recipient of Virginia's largesse. Somehow, Virginia was convinced that Ana loved her coffee.

Virginia constantly whistled as she moved about our apartment and as she walked up and down the stairs to the apartment. That fascinated Marsha, which led her to try to imitate her Aunt Virginia. She never quite succeeded. Virginia told us she whistled because she couldn't sing; since she grew up with a brother who whistled, she had joined him. (A note: Our girls, as well as the other missionary kids, had many aunts and uncles, such as Virginia. Because our biological families were so far away, all the missionaries became aunts and uncles to all the missionary children. We became family.)

I don't remember how long Virginia stayed with us, but I do remember that we enjoyed every minute of her visit — even if sometimes we had to refuse her coffee. Virginia loved our girls and the feeling was mutual. She loved the stool Marsha stood on to brush her teeth. These words were written on it in English: "Here I stand upon my stool, To practice every good health rule. Then my stool becomes a chair, To sit upon most anywhere." Virginia repeated the verse again and again.

Several years later, we visited Virginia in Rome. My sister Edna was with our family, so we planned to stay in a hotel. However, since the school that Virginia directed was closed for the summer, she had plenty of room for all of us. We even ate in the school dining room and had coffee – what else – with her in her apartment. We enjoyed our visit immensely.

Since Virginia towered over most Italians, we watched in fascination as she would put her hand out to stop traffic at intersections as we toured Rome. Traffic would come to a screeching halt, and we would follow meekly behind her like little ducklings. Then we learned that was the law in Italy: If a person steps into the street, traffic has to stop.

Many years later, Virginia and I shared in giving a report on missions in Europe at Ridgecrest Baptist Assembly in North Carolina. Gerald and I had arrived a little late for the meeting, so when I saw Virginia sitting three or four rows in front of us I wanted her to know we were there. I wrote "Here I stand upon my stool" on a piece of paper and sent it up to Virginia. She read it and exclaimed loud enough for everyone to hear, "The McNeelys are here." Thanks to Virginia, several hundred furloughing missionaries and personnel from the International Missional Board headquarters in Richmond knew we were there, too.

The next day, she was to speak first. I was surprised when she called me to the platform, but I thought she was going to explain our part on the program. Imagine my further surprise when she – almost six feet tall and strikingly beautiful – put her arm around all five-feet of me and said, "Well folks, this is the long and the short of it."

During our years in Spain, we hosted so many people that it would be impossible to begin to name them, much less write about what they meant to our family. One group, however, deserves special attention: the sailors from the American 6th Fleet.

❁

BARCELONA HAD BEEN the home port to three ships in the American 6th Fleet – headquartered in Naples, Italy – since 1951. Because Gerald had served in the U.S. Navy, he had a particular affinity with the sailors on those ships, and we both enjoyed visiting the ships and meeting the lonely American sailors. We were always glad to see them, and they were glad for a reminder of home. Sometimes some of the sailors came to church on Sunday evenings. On more than one occasion, I sat on the aisle end of a pew with two notebooks and a pen. As the pastor preached, I would translate the message and send it down the line. The sailors would read my translation and pass it on. Most of the sailors knew the hymns in English, so they would sing along in English as everyone else sang in Spanish. That brought smiles to many faces. Everyone enjoyed that.

I was often tired after a Sunday evening service, but most nights I still had to prepare supper – which was usually waffles and bacon. On many Sunday nights, we invited the sailors home with us to join in our family's Sunday night tradition. Gerald would set up our serving table and our waffle iron – which only made two waffles at a time – as I prepared the batter and fried bacon. One night after I'd made too many waffles to count, I was exceptionally tired and really wanted to quit cooking but instead I asked if everyone had had enough. All but one sailor said they had, so I made more waffles for the young man who wasn't yet satisfied. After he'd eaten a few more waffles, I asked if he hadn't yet had enough. He replied, "I can eat as many as you can make." Gerald then said, "Young man, we must think of the U.S. Navy. We don't want you to get sick." Everybody laughed and the sailor said he'd had enough. Thank goodness for Gerald. I'd made dozens of waffles that night and Gerald knew enough was enough.

Sometimes we'd get a telephone call telling us sailors would be at church at a certain time. They were usually officers. In those cases, I would prepare a full meal for them after Sunday night church. We enjoyed having them in our home.

Sundays weren't the only day sailors came to our home. We couldn't figure out how so many had learned about us until we heard that someone had put our address on a bulletin board in Italy with a note that said, "Where you can get Christian fellowship and good food." (Today, that reminds me of the mark those homeless, hungry, Depression-era men left on the gate of my parents' home in Kentucky – a mark telling their fellow travelers where they could find food.)

Since Gerald was often asked to conduct worship services on the ships, we felt an extra interest in the sailors. We were doubly blessed when a friend from our days at Georgetown College was in port. He was a chaplain. We were delighted to welcome him and his friends.

❀

IN OUR FIRST YEAR in Spain, I had the opportunity to travel out of the country by myself when I was invited to give two morning devotionals at a meeting of European Baptist women at the European Baptist Seminary in Rüschlikon, Switzerland. The invitation said something like, "You Americans are used to doing programs like this, so we would like you to come to Rüschlikon." At the time, Gerald and I had so many irons in the fire that I hesitated to go, but Gerald urged me to go since our seminary was on break and he could take care of the children as well as I could.

When I got home, I learned that all had gone well for Gerald and the girls until bath time. When a pail of water must be heated on the kitchen stove, carried down the hall, and then poured into the tub in order to have warm bath water, you learn to simplify. Gerald was used to heating the water and carrying it to me, but he always left the rest up to me. With me out of town, he would have to do it all. Gerald didn't want to complicate matters by getting the children's hair wet, so he asked Linda, "What does Mother do about your hair when she bathes you?" Linda replied, "She puts pins in our hair." Of course, I used bobby pins, but Gerald didn't know that, so he looked around for any kind of pins that he thought would do. Finally, he found some clothes pins, and the girls loved them. To this day, Linda still remembers how they laughed and wondered why Mother didn't do that. I think they were ready for Mother to take another trip because Daddy was so much fun.

The girls also loved to have their daddy read to them, too. I never understood why Daddy's reading was better than Mother's, especially since Mother was the librarian.

❖

THAT TRIP WAS JUST the first of many trips our family made to Rüschlikon over the years. As I became more proficient in Spanish, I was often asked to translate when we attended meetings there. The seminary was well-equipped with a number of translation booths so that several people could be translating into several languages simultaneously and attendees could use ear phones to listen. On one trip during our third term, I happened to be translating when the American evangelist Billy Graham was introduced. I hadn't looked at the program for the day, so I didn't know he was in Rüschlikon on his way to Scandinavia. I didn't have time to get nervous and was overjoyed to translate for him.

Imagine my surprise when a group from Portugal told me they had listened to my translation because they preferred listening to me instead of the Portuguese translator. They thought Portuguese speakers could understand Spanish much better than Spanish speakers could understand Portuguese!

❖

AS OUR FIRST TERM moved along, our family had much to learn about daily living. Because we were residents and not citizens, from our first days in Spain we were required to have our photo ID residency card on us at all times. The girls were included on my card – just as all Spanish children were included on their mothers' cards – and didn't have to carry residency cards. The ID was to be shown to any government official any time it was requested. Plus, all four of us were required to leave the country every six months. Most of the time, we simply crossed the border into France or went to tiny Andorra in the Pyrenees, had our cards stamped to show that we had crossed the border, and headed back to Spain. Sometimes, we'd enjoy a quick shopping trip in Perpignan or a meal in a French cafe.

I also had much to learn about women's fashions. Following the current fashions was important to Spanish women. Even if a woman didn't have many clothes, what she did have were the latest styles. One Easter, our helper wanted to make a dress and had saved up enough money for fabric but was having a problem deciding on a style. I tried to be helpful by offering her the latest Sears catalog to find an idea. She, however, found every dress in the catalog to be out of date. Finally, she found what she wanted in a French magazine at a local news stand. I offered her the use of my sewing machine but then realized she probably had never used one before. Instead, she made the dress entirely by hand, and it was perfect. Later, I noticed that she never left our apartment on her day off without wearing that dress. And she had been right about the style: It was the style all well-dressed women were wearing.

O LORD, our Lord,
how majestic is your name in all the earth!
Psalm 8:9

TEN

❀

We could hardly believe that we had been in Spain for four years and that it was time to make plans for our first furlough. In those days, Southern Baptist missionaries received a one-year-furlough after five years on the field, so we were very surprised when we were given a furlough after four years.

As Gerald and I prepared to go back to the States, our biggest concern was the transition to an American school system for Linda, who would be in fifth grade, and for Marsha, who would be in first grade. We worried about whether Marsha would refuse to speak English since she spoke only Spanish – even with Linda.

One day as we were rushing around getting things ready to leave, without thinking I said in English, "We're going home for a long time." Immediately, Marsha answered in Spanish: *"Pero ya estoy 'home.'"* Translated: "Home. I *am* home."

I told her that she needed to learn English before we got to the States and that as a first step we would speak only English at mealtime. Very emphatically, Marsha replied in Spanish, *"Puedo contar en Español Alemán y Frances. No lo voy aprender en Ingles."* Translation: "I can count in Spanish, German, and French. I am *not* going to learn English." When I explained that her first grade teacher in America wouldn't know those languages, she responded, *"Pues, que aprenda!"* Translation: "Well, let her learn." Stubborn Marsha. Wonder where she got that!

We did begin speaking English at mealtime. Marsha struggled with it, and Linda joined in by pouting a lot and sympathizing with Marsha.

There are an overwhelming number of things to do to prepare for furlough. You must plan to replace yourself so there is continuity in the work. Somebody had to be enlisted to teach Gerald's New Testament class. Somebody had to continue my library work. Since someone would be moving into our apartment, it had to be left presentable. Plus, we had to think about what we'd be doing in the States. We needed to collect materials to use as we shared about missions in Spain with churches, conferences, and camps. (And we had to remember that we would be speaking to people of all ages, from the very young to the old.) We also wanted to purchase gifts for family and friends, so some shopping was in order, too.

❀

BY 1962, AIR TRAVEL was possible for furloughing missionaries but it still was extremely expensive, so it was more practical for us to return to the States by ship. When our dear British friend and biblical scholar Dr. George Beasley-Murray learned that Gerald would be attending a conference of seminary professors at Spurgeon's College in London and travel to the States from there, he invited our family to be guests in his home. And so we drove together from Barcelona to London. Missionary Joe Mefford went with us in order to drive our car back to Spain.

We had a wonderful time. Gerald, Linda, Joe, and I enjoyed exploring London and Oxford. As for Marsha, she enjoyed staying at home with the Beasley-Murray children. Also, being in an all-English environment showed her just how much she needed to learn to speak English. Still, while we were in London, she continued to speak Spanish with Linda and me.

❀

CROSSING THE ATLANTIC on the Queen Elizabeth – I, not II – was quite different than our trip over on the Excaliber had been. Although our staterooms were well below deck, the ship was elegant and offered much to explore.

When we reached New York harbor five days later, the sight of the Statue of Liberty brought tears to our eyes. Marsha, however, was confused.

She had expected to see Ani and Mari at the docks. The two girls and their mother had been at the docks in Barcelona when we'd first arrived in Spain and had promised to be there when we returned from furlough. Unfortunately, Marsha thought they would meet us when the ship docked in New York. Maybe our trip to England and five days at sea seemed like a year to our six-year-old.

We flew from New York City to Louisville, which would be our home for the next year. We moved into missionary housing on the campus of Southern Seminary, which made it easy for the girls and me to walk to nearby Crescent Hill Baptist Church while Gerald was out visiting churches, telling about the work in Spain. (The girls and I often went with him, however.)

Living on campus also made it easy for me to spend time in the campus library to learn all I could about library work and for Gerald to take classes in his work toward a master of religious education degree. Because much of the religious education work in Spain was falling on his shoulders, he felt God leading him to be as prepared as possible. The girls attended a public school within walking distance of the seminary.

❀

OUR REUNION WITH family and friends was all that we had hoped. Of course, Marsha and Linda remembered very little about Kentucky, but they, too, felt the love in the welcome we received. Although Marsha had been too young to remember our extended family members when we'd moved to Spain four years before, she did recognize many of their names as we had always included them in our prayers.

We especially enjoyed reconnecting with friends in our former churches in Ewing, Mt. Zion, and Carlisle. How much we loved those people and how much we had learned from them!

And yes, Marsha continued to speak in Spanish. One day as she and I were walking down a street in Louisville, she said, *"Cuantos extranjeros hay aqui. Todo el mundo habla Ingles."* Translation: "There are so many foreigners here. Everyone is speaking English."

Eventually, she did learn English – but not without effort. One night after spending a day in first grade in a Louisville public school, Marsha said, "Today (pause) my teacher (pause) told me (pause) to make a *mariposa* [butterfly], but I didn't know how to make a (pause) *mariposa,* so I made (pause) *un árbol* [tree]." She was struggling, but at least she was trying.

Still, Marsha continued to speak Spanish when she was with Linda or Gerald and me. The girls often spoke Catalán, the language of the playground in Spain, especially when they didn't want us to understand them. Many years later, when Linda had married and had two children of her own, she often used a version of that trick on her children. Her daughter, Lisa, says that she and her brother, Matt, could always tell when their mother was really upset with them because she immediately switched from English to Spanish, which they didn't speak.

The girls did adjust to their new school and to speaking only English. Yet, it wasn't easy as both tended to be shy. Plus, few of their new peers had seen children who had lived outside the United States. In fact, most of their peers had never even heard of Spain and often would approach the girls to ask them to "talk in Spanish," which Marsha and Linda found both amusing and baffling.

As for their experiences on subsequent furloughs, both Marsha and Linda say that as teenagers the transition from Spain to Louisville and back to Spain was especially traumatic. Leaving friends behind – both in Spain and in Louisville – as well as making cultural adjustments was often painful. When Linda was sixteen, her piano teacher even offered to let her live with her in Barcelona instead of going on furlough with Gerald, Marsha, and me. Linda says she seriously considered the offer. (Of course, she went to Louisville. All wasn't lost because that was the year she met her future husband in a Louisville high school.) I guess other furlough secrets will have to wait to be told in the girls' memoirs.

❀

THROUGH THE YEARS, Gerald and I have been amused when people think a missionary furlough is a time for rest and relaxation. While the word *furlough* does imply time off, for missionaries returning to the States, it is far from that. The term *stateside assignment* which is used today is far more accurate. (I wonder if after furlough some missionaries needed a long ocean voyage to relax and decompress before arriving back on their field of service. When does one decompress when *flying* back to the field?)

On that first furlough and on each of our subsequent furloughs, our calendars filled quickly with opportunities to share about our ministry in Spain. On each furlough, we traveled thousands of miles. It was never a chore because we were telling the people who had sent us, had prayed for us, and whose monetary offering had made it possible about what God was doing in Spain.

❦

AFTER OUR SECOND term of service (1963-1967), we were eligible for a furlough after five years. By that time, air travel was affordable and we returned to the States by plane. For every furlough thereafter, we traveled by air.

Later, the Foreign Mission Board offered the option for more frequent, shorter furloughs for all missionaries. Shorter periods of time on the field can mean less disruption in the work of a missionary. That certainly was true for Gerald and me. In later years, three-or-four-month furloughs also allowed Gerald to work on and then earn his doctor of education degree from Southern Seminary. (He'd earned a master of divinity degree and a master of theology degree before we went to Spain. He'd also earned a master of religious education degree on our first two furloughs.) Shorter furloughs also allowed me to earn a master in library science degree from Spalding College in Louisville. And shorter furloughs meant that Gerald and I could spend more time more often with our grandchildren.

Our first three furloughs were year-long, but for the remainder we chose the shorter three-or-four-month ones. For all our furloughs except one, we lived in Louisville, which made it easier for Gerald to work on those additional degrees at Southern Seminary. For our first two furloughs, we lived in seminary missionary housing; for the third, we lived in the missionary house at St. Matthews Baptist Church.

After the girls had completed college in the States, Gerald and I spent a particularly delightful semester-long furlough at Georgetown College, our alma mater. We were there to help the children of missionaries (MKs or

Missionary Kids) from around the globe who were students at Georgetown adjust to living in the States.

We lived on campus in the college's missionary house, and although we focused on MKs we opened our home to all students who needed a sense of family. We talked with the students about their lives, their goals, and their personal decisions. And we had lots of fun. They consumed more brownies that I ever thought possible. Sometimes, some of the college's football players would come straight to our house after practice. On those days, open windows were a necessity.

❖

PREPARING TO RETURN to Spain took as much thought and planning as did preparing for furlough in the States. Selecting enough clothing for a family of four to wear until the next furlough was one of the biggest jobs. When we first went to Spain in 1957, very little ready-to-wear clothing was on the market there and what we did find was much more expensive than in the States. Plus, many Spanish families of means employed seamstresses, which was out of the question for us. At first, I did sew a few garments for the girls and myself but soon found I simply didn't have time for that. (In later years, Linda learned to sew and made many of her own clothes.)

And so, near the end of each of our furloughs as we prepared to return to Spain, one of my tasks was to select most of the clothing Gerald, the girls, and I would need until our next furlough. When there were four or five years between furloughs, that was quite a job. To this day, Linda and Marsha like to talk about how little enthusiasm they showed for this. Back in Spain, when a season changed, they and I would inspect the steamer trunks to see what I'd selected for them for that season. They always approached the trunks with some measure of fear and trepidation since what I'd chosen very well might not be to their liking. They also never knew whether what I'd chosen would still be in style.

I will praise you, O LORD, with all my heart;
I will tell of all your wonders.
I will be glad and rejoice in you;
I will sing praise to your name, O Most High.
Psalm 9:1-2

ELEVEN

❁

As our first furlough came to a close in the summer of 1962, we were
excited to be returning home to Spain. Yes, Spain was home. Gerald
and I were surer than ever of our call from God to work with the Spanish
people. Linda and Marsha were excited to be returning home to friends
and familiar surroundings.

We returned on the Exeter, the sister ship to the Excalibur on which
we'd made our first voyage in 1957. And yes, Ani and Mari Salvadó were
waiting on the dock to welcome Marsha home. How much better prepared
Gerald and I were when we arrived in Barcelona this time! We were ready
to hit the ground running, and the girls were ready to be back in a place
that was familiar, comforting, and filled with friends. They were more than
ready to pick up where they had left off. Plus, once again they could speak
Spanish whenever and wherever they wanted.

We moved into an apartment in a building in Barcelona on Avenida de
la Victoria. (A humorous aside: The street was named to celebrate the many
victories of Dictator Franco during the Spanish Civil War. After his death
in 1975, it was one among thousands of streets across the country whose
names were changed. During the years Franco was dictator, the main street
of even the tiniest *pueblo* had been named *Avenida Generalísimo Franco*.)
Our apartment was located between a medieval monastery and Finca Güell
of Antonio Gaudí, a residence that featured a dragon with a terrifying open
mouth on the front gate. Our apartment was unusual for Spain in that it
was on the ground floor. It also had a small basement room intended for a

live-in helper, but we'd stopped using helpers before we'd left for furlough because the cost had risen sharply.

Once again, Gerald and I were concerned about our girls' schooling. Because the Swiss School they'd attended only went through the sixth grade and Linda would be entering the sixth grade that year, we knew we'd soon have to begin looking for another school.

We considered a German school but rejected it because it was known to be very rigid. Someone even suggested that we send Linda back to the States. What to do? Gerald and I knew that God had called us to Spain. We were praying, so we knew He would help us decide what to do. We considered home schooling again, but I wondered how I could manage that along with my library work and other ministry responsibilities.

And then God answered our prayers. As Linda's sixth grade year was nearing its end, we received a letter from the American Consulate in Barcelona informing us that the consulate was considering opening an American school that would go through grade twelve. The consulate already had a list of talented teachers who were eager to come to Barcelona to teach. Relieved and thankful that God had answered our prayers, we immediately responded to say that the consulate could count on our girls as students.

After that, things happened rapidly. The school bought a large house and converted it into a school building. And so, the American School of Barcelona opened – just in time for Linda to enter seventh grade and Marsha to enter third grade. Granted, it was a private school but because we had no other option, the Foreign Mission Board covered the cost. An added bonus was that it was located near our apartment.

Both Linda and Marsha thrived in the American School. (All classes except language classes were in English, of course.) They enjoyed the diverse, multi-cultural experience the school afforded. Just as the Swiss School had been started by the Swiss but had a wide variety of countries represented in its student body, so the American School was started by the Americans but also had a diverse student body.

Of course, there were the usual school traumas. One day, a boy was trying to get Linda's attention on the playground when things got out of hand. Linda was always protective of her little sister and the boy knew that, so he picked up caterpillars from under the pine trees and threw them at Marsha, hitting her hand in the process. Her hand soon started to swell from an allergic reaction. It looked terrible. Thankfully, Gerald was at home and was able to take her to the hospital. She was given a shot and sent home. The large bandage she got may not have been necessary but it did make Marsha feel better. I think it made Linda feel even worse. After all, the boy had been trying to get her attention and Marsha was collateral damage.

Another day when Marsha was in the sixth grade, a teacher took several children on a school-sponsored excursion into the busy downtown streets of Barcelona. She took no aide or assistant with her, so as the group crossed a wide street the teacher went on ahead and told the children to follow her. Marsha was in the last group to cross the street when she fell, cut her head, and was bleeding. She was in pain, which set some of the other children to crying. The teacher said they would go to the hospital emergency room immediately. Then Marsha – banged up head and all – suggested that they should first go to the school because some of the children were still crying and she thought they should be taken care of before she was. The teacher agreed, took the children back to the school, and then took Marsha to the hospital. By the time we got the news, Marsha already had five stitches in her scalp. The teacher then called us from the hospital and brought Marsha home. The compassion Marsha showed that day was typical of her. We were used to seeing her put the needs of others before her own needs. That concern for children must have much to do with her becoming a children's counselor in her adult years.

In the eighth grade, Linda even started a school newspaper, the *Script,* which grew in content and sophistication as time went on. She also decided that the only way to conquer her stuttering was to volunteer for every oral report possible. This caused a lot of teasing and rolling of eyes from her classmates, but Linda was convinced that it would work. (Looking back in 2015, she says she doesn't know why she thought that would work.)

In 1965, when the school had outgrown its facilities, grades nine through twelve were moved to the sixth floor of the American Institute. (At the Institute, concerts, conferences, and English language classes were offered for the community.) Linda continued as editor of the school newspaper. She had several student-reporters who wrote news about things of interest to their fellow-students. Linda contributed illustrations and occasional articles and did the lay-out. Because none of them could type, I did all the typing. In those days, it was difficult to find a copy machine, so Linda and her staff often went from business to business, asking for free copy services. Linda continued the newspaper until she graduated.

❁

OUR SECOND TERM was busier that our first, if that was possible. Our calendars quickly filled with church responsibilities, seminary responsibilities, and family responsibilities.

As soon as we returned from furlough, we resumed the Sunday night youth fellowships in our home. Then Linda came up with the idea that the youth would appreciate having a Ping-Pong table. Gerald and I doubted that our tiny space could hold many Ping-Pong players, so Linda said the youth could take turns. As four played, she said, the others could crowd around the table and watch and wait their turn. When Gerald and I finally agreed, one problem remained: A Ping-Pong table would be expensive. Of course, Linda had an answer for that as well: A Ping-Pong table could be a Christmas present for both girls. Marsha agreed.

Gerald and I thought the girls fully understood that the Ping-Pong table would be their joint Christmas present until Marsha declared, "And you're going to put the presents downstairs on the Ping-Pong table." We did manage a few small presents after all.

The Ping-Pong table was a big hit. Before long, the youth were not only playing but also standing in line on the stairs, waiting their turn to play.

❁

THROUGHOUT OUR YEARS IN SPAIN, we often travelled to southern Spain to help churches with Sunday school training events. Whenever possible we took the girls with us to visit fellow missionaries and for some sight-seeing. We loved visiting with Tom and Betty Law and their four sons in Seville. In Granada, we visited the Bob and Jerry Worley family and toured the Alhambra many times. On the hillsides near Granada, we saw cave cities that made those hillsides look like beehives until we saw colorful cloths draped over the doorways and strings of electric lights circling from one door to another. In Guadix, we saw impressive chimneys rising from the ground, indicating that people lived down below. Later on, Gerald preached in a cave near Valencia when he and fellow missionary Joe Mefford were leading a service there.

Any time we were in the south of Spain, we just had to visit Córdoba, which was one of our family's special places. On one trip to Córdoba, I went into a *perfumería* – a shop that sold cosmetics and toiletries – while Gerald waited in the car with the car door wide open. As he sat there reading, a little boy with a shoe-shine kit approached him. *"No, los zapatos ya estan bien, no necesito un brillo."* Translation: "No, my shoes don't need shining," Gerald quickly told him. When he saw how dejected the lad was, he just as quickly said, *"Bueno, quizas lo necesitan."* Translation: "All right. You can shine them." As the boy shined his shoes, Gerald began a conversation with him and eventually asked him if he knew Jesus and if he would like to read a special book about Him. The boy replied, *"Pues, no puedo leer."* Translation: "No, I can't read." When he realized that Gerald planned to give him the little book he'd been reading, he added *"Pero mi madre lee un poco."* Translation: "But my mother can read a little." Gerald watched as the little boy walked away with that New Testament.

When Gerald told the girls and me about that little boy, we adopted him as one for whom we would pray frequently. Back at the seminary, Gerald told the students in his New Testament class about the little shoe-shine boy and they joined in our prayers. They also joined our family in praying for Córdoba and its 200,000 residents.

Then one of our favorite students, Antonio Gomez, said that God was calling him to Córdoba to start a church. After he finished his seminary training, he and his wife moved there and started with a small group that met in their apartment. For a long time, he looked for our little shoe-shine boy but could never locate him.

Many years later on a trip to Spain after we had retired, we saw Antonio and his wife. By then, their church had grown to be a large, active body of believers, and Antonio was still pastor. He hadn't found our shoe-shine boy – who by then would have been about fifty years old – but he was still looking.

On those family trips we also made sure we looked in on churches whose pastors and wives we'd come to know and love when they were students at the seminary in Barcelona. When we were able, we also checked in on some of the new church starts in remote areas.

❀

DURING OUR SECOND TERM we left the Bona Nova church to work with a church in Barceloneta, a fishing village that lies in a triangular tongue of land jutting into the Mediterranean Sea just below the Barcelona city center. At the time we went there, the village was known to be a rough area.

We'd decided to go there after a committee from the Barceloneta church told Gerald they needed him to attend a deacons' meeting to help them with a serious problem. At Gerald's first deacons' meeting he learned what the problem was: Several of the young women were wearing slacks to church. The deacons' wanted Gerald to tell them that slacks weren't proper attire for women in church. They told Gerald that the young people in the church already liked him and me and would listen to us. Gerald thought a minute and then told them that he would do what they had asked, but only on one condition: The deacons must wear long robes and sandals to church. That shocked them, but soon they began to laugh. That was the last time anything was said about women wearing slacks to church. Of course, the word got out and soon Gerald was even more popular with the young people.

❀

WHEN WE FIRST WENT to the Barceloneta church, attendance was low, so Gerald and I put on our thinking caps. We came up with an idea that we'd used on other occasions in other churches: fellowships. We knew that a popular event was coming up, so we decided to make the occasion a big deal. At the event, the traditional star attraction was for each person to bring a boiled sweet potato to church and eat it there. We told the people that I would bring extra food to share and to add to the sweet potatoes. Everyone loved the event. After that, it was easy to suggest that we have regular fellowships several times a month. Everyone loved the plan, and it was a big success.

For one of those fellowships, the women volunteered to bring desserts. I was very busy at the time and needed to bring something simple, so I made brownies. I knew the Spanish loved sweets and could buy elegant ones from the many bakeries across every city, so I wasn't sure how my brownies would go over. I needn't have worried – my simple brownies were a big hit. The people were intrigued by them. Fortunately, I'd baked enough for everyone to have at least one. They were fascinated by the name, too, and soon everyone had learned the English word "brownie." (For my brownies recipe, see Appendix 2.)

For special occasions at the church, I always baked and decorated a cake. As our gatherings grew, I had to bake bigger and bigger cakes. (I loved cake decorating and always supplied cakes for seminary events, such as graduations and piano recitals. I especially enjoyed making variations of an open Bible. Sometimes I'd add the seminary insignia, which made the cakes perfect for graduations. The most complicated cake I ever made was shaped like a grand piano with a bowl of flowers on top. I even made it to scale, measuring carefully so that all the keys were the right size and in the right place. Plus, it came complete with a piano bench. It was perfect for a piano recital.)

My cake baking and decorating led one of the church members who owned a small bakery to suggest that I work for him. He wasn't thinking I would bake and decorate *for* him but that I would become a partner *with* him in his bakery. Of course, I graciously declined the offer.

❈

MOST OF THE MEMBERS of the Barceloneta church were significantly poorer than those in the Bona Nova church. Sr. Cortes was an exception: He was a well-to-do builder. His wife was very attractive and dressed well, but simply. I doubt if many of the people in the church realized that her clothes were expensive because she never made that an issue. I also doubt if the church people realized how intelligent and how well educated she was. She never made that an issue, either.

On one occasion, we learned that some American naval officers from the Sixth Fleet planned to visit our church on a particular Sunday. When we told the church, a couple of the women asked to talk with Sra. Cortes and me. They told us that since we were expecting visitors they would like for us to dress up so the visitors wouldn't think that all the church members were as poor as they were. We complied. On the day the officers came, Sra. Cortes wore a fine fur coat that I'd never seen her wear before. I don't remember what I wore, but I do know I didn't have a fine fur.

Sr. Cortes was a deacon in the church and – like many deacons in Spain – he was a good preacher. One Sunday when our pastor was away Señor Cortes preached on crutches and with a cast on one foot and ankle. For his text, he chose 1 Peter 5:9: "Resist him [the devil], standing firm in the faith…." He told the congregation that he hadn't been standing firm the previous week when he was inspecting a house he was building. Everyone got a good laugh at that.

Our family had several unforgettable experiences with the Cortes family. One in particular stands out. One day when I was visiting in their home, their seven-year-old daughter, Miriam, came rushing in from playing on the street and started up the stairs. When her mother asked her where she was going, she said she had to get her Bible. Soon, she came running back down the stairs, Bible in hand. She paused long enough to tell us that a woman who didn't attend church was outside talking with the children and she wanted to tell her that if she came to church, she would learn about Jesus. Her mother just smiled and encouraged Miriam to go on outside. Then she told me that this was not unusual for Miriam and that she had marked several verses of Scripture in her Bible that she liked to share. Before long, that woman did come to church and brought her husband and sister with her. Soon after that, she and her sister made professions of faith in Jesus. Seven-year-old Miriam was a true *misionera* (missionary).

An elderly woman in the church also holds a special place in my heart. Sra. Pepita was fascinated with our girls because they were quiet and friendly with everyone in the church. While we were at Barceloneta, she made a beautiful handkerchief of fine needlework and gave it to Linda to save to carry in her wedding. Years later, Linda attached it to her wedding bouquet. And still later, Sra. Pepita made one for Marsha. By then her eyesight was failing and she couldn't crochet as well as before. It, too, was beautiful.

In time, one of our favorite seminary graduates, Don Luis Playa, became pastor of the Barceloneta church. Not long after that our family moved to Madrid. Before we left the Barceloneta church, Marsha emptied her piggy bank and gave the money to the pastor to use for youth activities. The pastor was so touched that he had tears in his eyes – which he didn't try to hide. He had known Marsha since she was two years old and they had become true friends. I'm sure he also remembered that when his wife had been in the hospital with the birth of their daughter, Marsha had taken most of the prize money she had won for a poem she'd written, bought an arrangement of his wife's favorite flowers, and had given them to her. Somehow, she'd known what her favorite flowers were. That was typical of Marsha.

❁

DENIA IS A BEAUTIFUL town along Spain's eastern coast between Valencia and Alicante that dates back to Greek and Roman times. With two sandy beaches, an ancient castle, and most of the houses made of white stucco with red tile roofs and patios trimmed in black wrought iron, Denia is a picturesque place. Add to that the vibrant, cheerful flowers and mosaic tiles seen everywhere and you get the picture of Denia. Plus, it's known for its own running of the bulls during the summer holiday of *Bous a la Mer* when bulls run into the sea. It also is known for its Jan. 06 celebration when the *Reyes Magos* – the Three Kings – arrive by boat and lead an elaborate parade of decorated floats complete with camels, horses, acrobats, and fire eaters through the town.

When we arrived in 1957, Spanish Baptists had owned seven acres in Denia for several years. The property was within walking distance of the Mediterranean Sea and was at the foot of Montgó Mountain. Spanish Baptists had wanted to build a camp/conference center on the property and yet by the time we arrived, they'd only been able to build a swimming pool and a small rustic dorm building. (For the inspiring story of the acquisition of the Denia property by Spanish Baptists, see Appendix 3.)

As national Woman's Missionary Union youth leader, I was excited to be in on planning our Spanish Baptists' first youth camp at Denia. Fellow missionaries Indy Whitten and Lila Mefford joined me as we got to work getting ready for camp. Lila and I cleared a place for a prayer garden, using a sickle. Even in Kentucky I'd never used a sickle, but Lila was a good teacher and I quickly learned.

For camp activities, we used natural rooms along the property line for small groups and Bible studies. Our walls were fig trees, almond trees, and other natural boundaries. A barbed wire fence made a perfect perch for my poster displays. The camp's three-sided concrete outdoor kitchen proved no hindrance to the preparation of some amazing meals, especially when Señora Maria was at the helm.

We decided to set up army surplus pup tents in the open field that was used for soccer and other types of recreation. We planned for the older girls to sleep there, two to three in each tent. We decided the younger girls could sleep in bunk beds in the one small dormitory building on the property. We thought we'd prepared well and had plenty of bunk beds until girls kept coming and coming. What could we do? We decided to shove the bunk beds together to make room for three girls instead of two, which meant that one girl would have to sleep in the crack between beds. The girls were delighted and thought the whole arrangement added to the camping experience. Indy and I decided we'd sleep in the pantry.

Sleep, however, wasn't the operative word. Pass the night was a better description. Before we settled down, I went to check on the younger girls in their bunk beds. Most were still awake. When I found Marsha, she was nestled in the crack between her friends Ani and Mari. When I went over to kiss her and her friends goodnight, I started something. All the girls wanted kisses. That night I kissed forty little girls. Then I went back to the pantry and fell asleep.

My sleeping didn't last long. First, two girls were sure a nest of spiders was under their tent, so Indy and I took the tent down in the dark. Those girls crawled into another tent. Then the night became very windy and a tent broke and fell. What to do? Fortunately, one of our workers had a needle and some heavy thread, so Indy and I sewed up the tent by flashlight. Linda was in another tent and witnessed the entire thing. I'm not sure I slept that entire night. Each night thereafter I paced among the tents several times with a flashlight. Even when I was in the pantry, I watched the tents from the window next to my cot. Thankfully, everything worked out fine after that first night.

Gerald and Charles Whitten and his son, David, were also involved in that Denia camping experience. Each day, Gerald drove to several farms in the area, looking for fresh fruits and vegetables to buy. David played his accordion each morning as the girls' wake-up call.

As for Spanish Baptists' dreams for a more permanent retreat center, thanks to funds from the Lottie Moon Christmas Offering given by Baptists across the United States, in the early 1960s they were finally able to construct a large camp building as a retreat center. Over the years many church leaders were trained there, and many youth were challenged to live out their faith while attending camp there. It also became the perfect place for mission meetings – those times when the American missionaries from across Spain came together for fellowship, inspiration, and to conduct business.

For our family, Denia still holds a special place in our hearts. For Marsha, it is indeed a very special place as she came to faith in Jesus at Girls' Auxiliary camp in Denia when missionary Uncle Charles Whitten was preaching. She remembers that his strongly Mississippi-accented Spanish didn't stand in the way of more than twenty girls – including her – from all over Spain asking the Lord to be their Savior that day.

Be still, and know that I am God;
Psalm 46:10a

TWELVE

✿

When we returned to Spain in 1968 for our third term of service, once again we hit the ground running. Family responsibilities, church responsibilities, and seminary responsibilities made for a full schedule. Additionally, the Vietnam War was in full swing and protests seemed to be all around us.

Having ships from the American 6th Fleet docked in Barcelona harbor had become a contentious issue as U.S. action in Vietnam was seen by many Spanish people as cruel and unwarranted. And having three ships docked at one time – just waiting to be called into action – was in itself incendiary. In fact, anything associated with the United States became the target of protests.

The American High School where Linda was a senior was often a target. Young protesters took out their frustrations by throwing stones at the building, which had a glass front. On many days, classes had to be held in the hallway because of broken glass in the classrooms. We regularly saw overturned cars, burned-out vehicles, and other signs of protest in the city.

✿

IN HER FINAL year of high school, Linda also attended the University of Barcelona and completed a Certificate of Foreign Studies, a degree that was used in some European countries as a teaching degree. She focused on Spanish literature, Spanish history, ancient art of Spain, and modern art of Spain – the modern art era began in 1492. Gerald and I had earned that certificate, too.

Adding studies at the University of Barcelona meant Linda spent two hours each school day at the American High School before taking a bus and the Metro (subway) to the medieval university. She returned home at nine p.m. An independent spirit, Linda loved it. She travelled to parts of Barcelona that her father and I rarely saw. Plus, her studies gave her many credits that transferred to an American college the following year.

That year Linda spent a lot of time riding public transportation, and she used the time wisely. Often she left evangelistic tracts on the bus or subway. Surrounded by a huge crush of people, sometimes she would read a tract as she travelled, and when she did invariably there would be a head or two popping over her shoulder to read along with her – the Spanish have a different concept of personal space than Americans. Sometimes she would point to a particular sentence or paragraph and start a conversation. In spite of the ever-present Vietnam protests, she experienced no problems.

Linda also continued as editor of the American High School newspaper. While on furlough, she had worked on her school's newspaper in Louisville, so she had a clearer idea of what to do to make a more interesting paper. When she returned from furlough, she pulled the troops/reporters back together and they got to work. This time around, she was the person who went to businesses to sell advertising for the paper. One day the principal of the American High School received a call from a business person who had bought advertising from Linda. He asked: "Who was that girl who came here representing the school? She walked into my office and shook my hand!"

Linda graduated from the American School in June 1969. In her graduating class of twelve were an Australian, a Filipino, a Chinese, a Swiss, a Spaniard, a Brit, and three Americans – including Linda. As Linda was concluding her valedictory address, a fellow missionary sitting beside me whispered, "Did you notice that Linda didn't stutter once during the whole address?" It was true. All her years of volunteering for oral reports and facing the jeers and laughter of classmates was finally paying off.

❀

IN JULY 1969, Linda left for college in the States. She had chosen a Baptist girls' school in Mississippi because one of our fellow missionaries had gone there and suggested it. Gerald and my only objection was the location, which we felt was too far from home – meaning Louisville. In retrospect, we shouldn't have told her that. For Linda, home was Spain.

That first year Linda recorded all her expenditures in a little book Gerald and I had given her. We wanted her to get used to taking on that responsibility. She kept it faithfully for the first year, even writing down every snack and every issue of *Seventeen* magazine she bought. We knew her study habits were good, so we didn't worry about that.

We also knew Linda had a good spiritual foundation and we trusted her to depend on the leadership of the Holy Spirit. She had made her public profession of faith at Carlisle Baptist Church on our first furlough. The night before, we had been staying at our friends the Neals' home when Linda, Gerald, and had I knelt by the bed and prayed together.

Looking back, Linda says she knew that when she left Spain for college in the States, she wouldn't have us with her nor would she have much contact with us. She knew she would have to start figuring out what God's will was for her personally, outside our family circle. Her relationship with the Lord would have to be one that she could utterly depend on and that wouldn't let her down. She says she also knew for her a decision to follow Christ would be one of complete surrender.

In that first year of college, Linda also learned first-hand just how long ten days is as it still took that long for a letter to cross the Atlantic. She often said that if she had a problem at school and she wrote home about it, by the time our response reached her that problem had been solved and she was on to the next crisis. That year, a Woman's Missionary Union group gave her a much-appreciated gift: money to make a phone call to Spain. She saved that call for Christmas; she knew the school year would be half over then and that would be her only call of the year.

After a year in Mississippi, Linda transferred to Georgetown College – her parents' alma mater – and finished her college degree there. She majored in Spanish and minored in English. She also had enough hours in French to qualify as a minor.

❀

THE YEAR LINDA left for college Marsha began ninth grade at the American High School. The Vietnam War protests continued and intensified alarmingly. One day, nearly 500 university students demonstrated outside the American Institute where the school was located. They threw stones and chunks of concrete that they'd broken from the pavement in front of the door. They broke windows on the first, second, and third floors. It was a scary time for Marsha and her fellow students. They knew they couldn't all leave the school at the same time, so they left in groups of twos and threes.

That day Marsha brought several classmates home with her because they were too scared to go to their own homes. Later that evening, Gerald drove them all home. That day the protesters also broke windows at other buildings in Barcelona that housed American interests.

❀

AT THE AMERICAN School, Marsha was known for her generosity. For example, we had two good sets of encyclopedias at home and Marsha freely lent volumes to anyone who asked – even if she needed them herself. How do parents deal with a fault like that? Gently, Gerald and I tried to tell her that it wasn't selfish to think of her own needs for those books even when someone else asked to borrow them. When Marsha left for college in the States, Gerald and I went to the American School to collect missing volumes that she'd lent out. At that time, we were preparing to move to Madrid and preferred to move with two complete sets of encyclopedias.

Marsha was also known for her honesty and compassion. One teacher told Gerald and me that when she needed to send lunch money to the office, she always trusted Marsha to take it because she never doubted Marsha's honesty. She also said that any time a new student came to the school she knew Marsha would take him or her under her wing and help the student get adjusted.

One such student was Yael from Israel. Yael didn't speak any of the languages any of the students or teachers spoke; she spoke only Hebrew. So the teacher called on Marsha to help, even though she didn't speak Hebrew either. That didn't seem to matter as Marsha was quickly in her element. Somehow she invited Yael to our home for a sleepover. I can still see pretty little Yael sitting on the top bunk in Marsha's room, laughing. She seemed to enjoy everything even though she couldn't understand anything the other girls were saying. That wasn't Marsha's only sleepover; in fact, we called her sleepovers mini-United Nations as there were always girls from Spain, North and South America, Sweden, Israel, and many other countries. Gerald and I never knew who or what to expect at Marsha's sleepovers.

The only time I remember Marsha being invited to anyone's home was to visit with two sisters from Sweden. Marsha even brought home a recipe of a dish she'd particularly enjoyed, which made her very popular with the girls' mother. That Swedish meatballs recipe turned out to be almost identical to the one I always used.

With Linda gone, Marsha enjoyed experiences that were uniquely hers. Once while we were attending the week-long post-Easter festival called Feria in Sevilla, fellow missionary Betty Law suggested that we outfit Marsha in a true Sevillana Flamenco costume. (Betty had four boys and had always wanted a girl, so Marsha became hers for the night.) While Feria is celebrated in cities across Spain, the celebration in Sevilla is one of the most spectacular. That night Betty decked Marsha out in a flounced dress of navy with white dots and red ruffles around all the edges. To make the outfit even more authentic, we added a rose, *peineta* (comb), bracelets, and earrings. Marsha looked lovely and thoroughly Spanish. As I looked around at the crowd of people, I saw that almost every girl from toddler on up was wearing a flounced dress with *mantón* (an intricately hand-embroidered scarf with fringe) over the shoulder. Traditionally, only unmarried women wore *mantones*, but that night it seemed to me that hundreds of women of all ages were wearing them. Surely they weren't all single.

The next day the festivities continued with a parade of horses, ridden in traditional Spanish style. Some men and a few beautiful girls dressed in leather riding habits rode alone, but others rode on their horses in *parejas* (pairs). Often, tiny children – who also were dressed up – rode with the *parejas*. Everywhere we looked, people young and old were dancing together. We watched as three year-olds and four-year olds danced with adults. Marsha dressed in her Flamenco outfit that day, too. Plus, we added a Córdoba hat to her outfit. Traditionally, one doesn't wear the comb or the rose with the hat; instead, one wears a red carnation behind one ear. And of course, that's what Marsha did.

❀

OVER THE YEARS we lived in Spain we attended many Spanish Baptist churches. Some of the buildings were elegant in their simplicity. Such were Bona Nova Baptist and Barceloneta Baptist in Barcelona and First Baptist in Madrid. Other newly-started churches, however, had to be creative in finding meeting places because of limited finances.

One church met in a former chicken coop. The members didn't have much money to turn the building into a church, so they made light fixtures out of large tuna fish cans, poking holes in the sides of the cans to let light through. I was told they borrowed the idea from a church in the Canary Islands.

One Sunday evening Gerald preached there, so he was seated on the small platform at the front. The tiny church was packed, and when Linda, Marsha, and I came in, we were taken to the front row of seats. At first I was embarrassed but soon was grateful to be so near the platform. That night the weather was very hot, so the fact that the now-church building had once been a chicken house was more evident by the minute. On top of that Gerald was very tired; I was afraid he would fall asleep before it was time for him to preach. Spanish evening services often begin as late as 9 p.m. and sometimes last a long time, so I knew he could be sitting on that platform a very long while. So I had to get creative. As I sat in that front pew in my high heels, I would swing my foot so Gerald could see it. It must have worked because he didn't fall asleep and he preached a good sermon.

On another occasion we visited a church that met in the pastor's living/dining room. The large room was packed with people sitting in folding chairs. That day Gerald wasn't preaching, so the four of us sat about halfway to the front. As the service progressed we noticed three or four little boys in the front row who were becoming restless and had started giggling. Finally, the pastor had all he could take, so he went over to the boys and slapped one of them – we learned later that was his son. That stopped the mischief. You couldn't have seen quieter boys after that.

❋

IN 1968 GERALD became interim director/president of the *Seminario Teológico Bautista* after director/president Russell Hilliard became ill. Then in 1970 Gerald was appointed president.

Board members were enthusiastic about Gerald becoming president, so much so that the first thing the board chairman said to him was, "And now we want you to move the seminary to Madrid."

The field is the world.
Matthew 13:38

THIRTEEN

❀

For several years, Baptists in Spain had considered the possibility of moving their seminary to the capital city of Madrid, a city of 3 million people. They felt that if the seminary moved from Barcelona in the far northeastern part of the country to the center of the country then students would could more easily reach any point in Spain. That would boost Spanish Baptists' efforts to start churches in unreached areas and to provide preachers for the many small groups and congregations that were forming across the country. While Barcelona had been home for the first years of the seminary, they felt it was time for a move. And so Spanish Baptists had begun making plans to move *Seminario Teológico Bautista* to Madrid.

As I wrote in chapter twelve, in the same board meeting in 1970 in which Gerald was named president, board members voted to move the seminary to Madrid. While we knew the move was coming, we didn't expect it to be so soon. Gerald rose to the challenge. Much of the responsibility for the logistical details of the move fell on his shoulders. Over the next months, he made the eight-hour journey from Barcelona to Madrid many, many times. He and a committee of Spanish Baptist leaders went to Madrid to look for a building site and to select an architect and a builder. They chose a site in Alcobendas, a northern suburb. Gerald guided the purchase of the property, the designing of a building plan, and the actual construction of the building. Gerald also had to find rental housing for the seminary students and their families.

While the building was under construction, for the first year the seminary held classes in a Baptist church and for the second year, it met in a rental property. Even before the building was complete, we moved in and began classes. Nuns at the parochial school next door offered to let us tap into their electricity, and we gratefully accepted.

When the time came for the move from Barcelona, most of the missionaries were out of the country and even most of the Spanish faculty and staff were away, so Gerald was responsible for the move, too. I insisted on packing the library myself; I wanted to be sure it would be easy to organize the stacks when I unpacked. That turned out to be a wise decision because when I got to Madrid I was the only person available to unpack. By that time we'd acquired thousands of books, so it was no small task.

To help pay for the new facility, Spanish Baptists used the building for several purposes in addition to seminary classes. It housed the office of the Spanish Baptist Union – the national organization of Baptists; the office of the Baptist Mission to Spain – the Southern Baptist missionaries; and the office for the Bible Correspondence Course. In essence, it was the Baptist Center Building. The seminary occupied half of the two-story building. The top floor held small apartments for single male and female students.

❦

IN THE MEANTIME Gerald and I had found a place to live in the rapidly developing Plaza Castellana area of Madrid. We rented an apartment in central Madrid for two years in order to live near the temporary quarters of the seminary. When the seminary building was completed enough to be used, we moved near the property. We felt the apartment that we'd found would be perfect for our needs. We would be able to walk to the seminary, which was important since we would be on different schedules and our mission board provided only one car for us. We also expected to be hosting company constantly, so we felt we needed to have a guest room always at the ready. Thankfully, we found just what we needed: two adjacent apartments that could easily be converted into one by removing the wall between them. That would give us plenty of room for guests.

Shortly after moving into the apartment, an American pastor came to visit. We later learned he had come to "see how missionaries really live".

He was a large man – to say the least—which presented a problem when he first arrived and the electricity went off in the building. That meant the elevator was down and he and Gerald had to walk up five flights of stairs to get to our apartment. Of course, Gerald graciously carried our guest's luggage up those stairs. Even though the man had to stop to rest several times, he didn't complain once.

That night the electricity was still off, but I was able to prepare a candle-lit dinner on our gas range. When bedtime came, the electricity was still off. Our guest had to use a candle in a candle holder to make his way to his bedroom. Thankfully, when we awoke the next morning, the electricity was on.

As I wrote in chapter six, we'd adjusted well to apartment living. We did, however, get some complaints about Gerald's piano playing when we lived in Madrid. And there was the downstairs neighbor there who often complained that I used the clothes washing machine too much – she must not have noticed how many overnight guests we had. Nothing changed with her even after I'd helped her daughter with English after she failed her English exam. Still nothing changed when the daughter passed the second exam and got a job that required English. And still nothing changed when she met an American airman through that job, married him, and moved to the United States. Her mother still complained.

❧

AS FOR MARSHA, she spent her junior year at the American School of Madrid among students from about fifteen countries. It was a challenging year for her in that she was one of only two believers (Christians) in the entire school.

While Marsha often said she was happy to finally be the only child at home, I wasn't so sure. One day she had us stop at a roadside market to buy a large, Texas style hat, which she put on the car seat where Linda would have been sitting had she still been at home. She missed her big sister.

❧

IT TOOK SEVERAL years for the seminary building to be completely finished, though we made good use of it even in the final construction phases. Of course, in addition to overseeing the construction, Gerald continued teaching as well as performing his duties as seminary president. And often, when the grass around the building was getting too tall, Gerald could be seen with his scythe, whacking the tall grass. That was one way to help keep expenses in check. I was busy equipping a new library. Soon, however, we both would add even more to our schedules.

In Barcelona, the seminary had no set plan for women's studies. Instead, what was offered depended on who was available to teach and what that person wanted to teach. Most often, missionary wives did the teaching, and the subjects they taught varied widely.

After we moved to Madrid, Gerald changed that. It was decided that the classes for pastors' wives needed more structure and that they needed to be Bible-based or at least be something the women could use as pastors' wives. Gerald and I worked out a simple, practical plan of study for the women. We decided the women could study Old Testament one year and New Testament the next. The third year we would concentrate on practical studies such as how to teach children. Also, the women could study English with their husbands if they desired to do so. It was a great plan, except for one thing: I was the only available teacher. And so we decided that I could take an hour each day from my library work, do my course preparation and grading of papers at night, and teach the courses myself. I didn't plan to teach the English class, as Esther Borrás was already doing that.

Still, there was one more problem to be solved before we could set our plan in motion. Because no missionary would be available to keep the nursery for the preschoolers of my students, we would need to find a young woman to take care of the children while their mothers were in class. We found the perfect person in Chari Nuñez, a young woman who had studied in the U.S. We paid her a salary and rented a small apartment for her. Chari became an older daughter for Gerald and me. We truly loved her. She even stayed with us for several months before moving to her own apartment.

Most of the women in my classes had no previous school experience beyond elementary school, so understandably they were very nervous when exam time came. I wasn't sure how to help them, but then the women themselves came up with a perfect idea. Previously, I'd made some candy for a school function and brought the leftovers to share it with the women. They loved the candy. So, one of the women suggested I make some to help them relax during the exam. It worked.

That, however, created another problem: A couple of the men said they were jealous and needed candy for their exam, too. So I made the men the same kind I'd made for the women. The day the men took their exam, they were delighted with the homemade candy – all but one man, that is. He even laughed at the others and at the very idea of having candy at an exam. And so I simply put the dish of candy on the arm of a chair in the middle of the room so the men could take a piece whenever they wanted. Finally, the man who thought the candy was silly decided to try a piece. He walked over to the dish, took a piece and ate it as soon as he returned to his desk. We all could hardly contain our chuckles when we saw him return for another piece of candy. After that, he moved his desk up close to the candy dish. There were smiles all around. He didn't seem to notice the smiles. He really liked the candy.

As it turned out, one year I was the only person available to teach English to the seminary students and their wives. I added teaching English to my agenda.

❁

BECAUSE THERE WAS no Baptist church in Alcobendas, the logical thing to do was to use the seminary building and its one main room to begin a church. The church got off to a slow start, which we'd expected. Sometimes, there was just Gerald and me. I teased Gerald that on those Sundays he preached to me and I taught the Sunday school lesson to him.

We knew that eventually we would have a ready audience in the wives and children of our seminary students. Because they didn't own cars, the men would be traveling by train to preach all over Spain on Sundays and they wouldn't be able to their families with them. It would simply be too expensive. And so those wives and children became the nucleus of the new church.

Gerald became the unofficial pastor and immediately began thinking about people living in the Alcobendas area who might be interested in coming to the church. One of the families he contacted had three daughters who were happy to find a church so close to their home; they would no longer have to take the long bus ride to a church in central Madrid. (At the time, there were five or six Baptist churches in Madrid, a city of three million people.)

Gerald also began playing softball with the neighborhood kids on Saturdays in order to get to know them. At one point he coached two teams at the same time and played on the teams when necessary. It made for exhausting Saturdays for a middle-aged man. But it was worth it as neighborhood kids began coming to church and bringing their families and their friends. Gerald especially remembers the Herreras family. Soon after several of the boys began playing on the softball teams, all ten members of the Herreras family began coming to church. Then they began inviting their friends. The church was off to a great start.

Gerald often asked students who didn't have a commitment in another church to preach in the Sunday service. When that happened, Gerald stayed in the nursery. The children loved him and were happy to have him all to themselves. One day I went to the nursery and found Gerald sitting on the floor with tiny children climbing all over him. Apparently that wasn't unusual.

❖

WE HAD MANY wonderful experiences at the Alcobendas church. I remember two beautiful young sisters who came to the church for the first time one Sunday evening. That night I was the only person there as all the other members had gone to a special program in another church. I'd chosen to stay behind because I knew it was always possible that someone whom we'd invited might drop in. I'm glad I did. That night I knew God had sent Margarita and Angelina to hear about Jesus, so I told them about Him. They asked many questions and that night they both accepted Jesus. The next Sunday they came back to church and made public professions of faith. They were two happy young girls and were some of our first members.

Sometime later I saw Angelina talking with several young adults. She ran over to me and said, "I'm trying to make you a grandmother!" I didn't understand. "I'm telling them about Jesus! Since you won me to Jesus, I'm trying to do the same for these neighbors. That way I will be *their* spiritual mother," and I would be their grandmother. Margarita made me promise to say *"Gracias"* to anyone in the States who had a part in sending me to Spain.

Drama became an important part of the church's ministry. Even as Gerald and I had done so many years before in our churches in Kentucky, we had to get creative. We closed the divider that was used to create two classrooms from our one large room and used the smaller of the two rooms as a stage. We turned the seminary desks around and made a fairly large space for our theater.

I found some dramas written for children and set to work. We began with the children of our seminary students but soon were able to invite children from the neighborhood to participate in our plays. The parents of those children often came when we put on the plays. On those occasions, Gerald always offered a brief devotional. In time, those plays came to be a good source of members for our new church.

Spanish children are natural-born actors, so it wasn't difficult to get them to participate in drama. Since it was the custom of Spanish Baptist churches for children to recite poems for Mother Day and other special days, appearing before an audience was not new to many of them. Even tiny toddlers would participate, often saying just two lines. I worked many of their *poesias* (poems) into the play programs. The recitation of the poems was so well received that many parents came just to hear their children recite.

On Mother's Day one year we had a children's program at the church that included the children reciting their *poesias*. That time we also had planned a special treat. Gerald, Marsha, and I had recently returned from furlough in Kentucky and had come back to Madrid with a new toy – a Polaroid camera. On that furlough as we were visiting friends in Northern Kentucky, our host had shown us a Polaroid camera that he'd recently purchased. That had given me an idea and I told Gerald we needed to buy one. Instead, our friends bought one for us.

147

Now back in Madrid, I was ready to put my idea into motion and my new camera to work. And so at our Mother's Day celebration, we took a picture of each child reciting their *poesia* and placed the instant pictures in specially prepared envelopes complete with ribbons tied on a corner. As the first girl left the stage, we handed her an envelope and told her to give the envelope to her mother. She did, plus she gave her mother an added bonus – a kiss. The recitations continued. Amazingly, all the children followed the first little girl's example and presented their mothers with the envelope – and a kiss. Even teenagers followed the example of the little ones. Of course, all the mothers loved it!

The plays continued to be so popular that at a few of the performances there wasn't enough room for everyone who attended. On those occasions, parents and friends of the children who appeared early in the program would leave their seats after their children had performed and go into the entrance hall to make room for the parents of the children who would perform later.

Some of the plays were serious, and I used the older youth in those. One time an older teenager asked to take part in a play, so I gave him a small part. The young man worked hard. When the time came for him to say his few lines he did fine – except for one detail. When he'd finished his part, he looked into the wing where I stood ready to prompt anyone who needed help and asked, *"Lo hice bien?"* Translation: "How did I do?" That brought no laughs or jeers from the audience because everyone knew and cared about Josete.

Josete attended church regularly, so we hadn't been surprised when he made a profession of faith and asked to be baptized. After the baptism, Gerald told Josete that he needed to show his sincerity by inviting others to come to church in order that they could have an experience like he had. He took that seriously and started by inviting his mother. Soon he was bringing someone new with him on many Sundays. One Sunday, however, Josete didn't come to either Sunday school or worship. And then the following Sunday, he didn't come again. The next week, however, he did come and brought a young boy with him. When Gerald asked him why he hadn't been in church the previous two Sundays, Josete simply explained, "I didn't have anybody to bring."

Very soon I ran out of prepared dramas, so I began to write them myself, often using Scripture as a base. For example, when my Sunday school class of teenagers was studying about Moses, I wrote a play around him. Our teenage actors were completely engaged not only in learning and performing but also in making props and background scenery. (A covered step-ladder next to other covered objects became the mountain from which Moses could look into the Promised Land.) But perhaps the most important thing that happened was that when we worked on plays built around biblical people, the teens had to read and reread the biblical passages about those people.

Summer Vacation Bible School (VBS) was a huge event at Alcobendas. Every day, Gerald even ran a taxi service to pick up four carloads of children. Each day, VBS ended with the children singing, *"La escuela se termina, nos vamos al hogar."* Translation: "School is over, now we're going home."

❊

THROUGHOUT ALL OUR years in Spain, Vacation Bible School was always one of my favorite ministries. Some of my most precious memories come from VBS experiences.

At one church I was assigned to work with six, seven, and eight-year-olds. I'd planned carefully and was glad to see that a woman whom I enjoyed being with was going to be my assistant. We'd planned for her to teach a character story and for me to teach a Bible story each day. We'd also planned accompanying appropriate learning activities, along with music, games, and recreation for the VBS that would run from Monday through Friday.

Unfortunately, I woke up on Monday with a severe case of laryngitis. I gargled, took medicine, and rested my voice as much as possible. Gerald suggested I call someone to take my place but I didn't know anyone who wasn't already teaching in VBS. I kept hoping I'd soon be able to talk normally. I thought about asking Gerald to pinch-hit but I knew he had other more pressing responsibilities. I would have to struggle through myself.

That day my assistant did a fine job telling the character story, and then it was time for my Bible story. I still couldn't talk normally and instead almost whispered. The result surprised me. In our discussion of the story after I had finished, all the children whispered, too!

In one VBS, a little girl in my class was filthy and gave off a noticeable odor. At the end of the day as the class sat together in a pew the other children made a point of moving as far away from the little girl as possible. All but one boy, that is. We'd just studied about Paul, using drama to teach the story, and that boy had played the leading role. It was the story in Acts 9 about how the disciples were afraid of Paul after his conversion and wouldn't let him join in their group. Then after Barnabas assured them that Paul was now preaching about Jesus, they accepted him into their group. As my young student sat near that little girl, I heard him repeat to himself, *"Yo era Pablo. Yo era Pablo."* Translation: "I was Paul." The story, in the form of a drama, had impressed him so much that he felt responsible.

Just before we left Spain in 1989 for retirement, I had a VBS experience that is indelibly etched in my mind and heart. To this day, I can easily re-create the scene.

That summer I'd been directing Vacation Bible Schools in several churches when a pastor, with sadness in his voice, said to me, "I wish I had someone to help me have Vacation Bible School in my church." Although Gerald and I were already packing to return to the States, I asked him, "Have you asked anyone?" "No," was his answer. "Well, here I am. Ask me," I replied. He seemed surprised and asked, "Would you really help me? You're getting ready to return to the U.S.?" I again replied, "Ask me and see." We had a wonderful VBS.

One child in that VBS especially touched my heart. One day I heard a knock on the church door. When I went to the door, I saw an attractive boy who appeared to be about ten years old. I welcomed him and then he asked, *"Puedo venir a su escuela?"* Translation: "Can I come to your school?" I told him he would be most welcome. He showed me a few coins and said, *"Es todo el dinero que tengo."* Translation: "But this is all the money I have." I assured him that he didn't need money for this school because it was a special one where we studied the Bible. That made him happy, so he joined us. Then he said he couldn't read and asked if we would still want him in our school. I said we would. At break time, I registered him and learned

CALLED! STEP BY STEP

his name was Antonio. When it was time for refreshments and the other children began lining up, Antonio stayed by my side. When I asked him if he wanted to join the children, he said, *"No puedo. Es todo el dinero que tengo."* Translation: "I can't. This is all the money I have" and showed me his coins again. When I told him he didn't have to pay for the refreshments, he surprised me by quickly running into the street to a popcorn stand and bought me some popcorn. Then he got in line for refreshments.

Before Antonio left the church that day, I asked him if he had a friend whom he could bring with him the next day. The next day he brought a little boy name Jesús with him. (*Jesús*—pronounced He-sus – is a popular name for Spanish boys.) When I sought to register Jesús, he didn't even know his name or address. Even though Antonio had said Jesús and he were the same age, Jesús was much smaller. To get Jesús' attention while I was asking him his name and address, I put my arm around him. He instantly snuggled up to me as he continued to look around, and I noticed that he smelled badly. I wondered if he'd ever been in such a large building and seen so many happy children. He told me he'd never been to school, so he'd never learned to read. I also wondered if he'd ever been shown affection since at refreshment time he seemed torn between wanting cookies and staying with me.

Later I asked Antonio if he knew Jesús' address. That's when I got a big shock. Antonio told me that Jesús didn't have a home. "He sleeps under the delivery wagon across the street. If the weather is cold, he's allowed to sleep in the doorway of the apartment house where his boss lives," Antonio said. Jesús' job was to carry bags of food for animals. Antonio also told me that all Jesús had to eat were the leftovers his boss gave him, which weren't much. Obviously, Jesús' boss was taking advantage of a homeless child. Antonio also said that sometimes his own mother would let him bring Jesús home with him.

As Antonio continued to tell Jesús' story, I was feeling worse by the minute. I wished I could take Jesús home with me, but I knew that was impossible. Gerald and I were in the middle of packing to retire in the United States. All I could do that day was see that Jesús left with some food.

The next day both Antonio and Jesús were at church early. The first thing I noticed was that Jesús had tried to wash his face. I saw that he'd washed only what he could see in a mirror. He'd tried to wash his hands, too, but had only made it up to his wrists. I knew immediately he'd gone to a public restroom to try to wash up. How many times could my heart be broken for one child?

Meanwhile, we were preparing for our last trip in Western Europe as well as trying to decide what we would take to the States with us when we left our beloved Spain. In a day or two we would drive to Zaragoza and pick up our missionary-friends, Howard and Joyce Clark, and together we would drive to Hungary.

On that trip I continued to think and pray for little Jesús and for Antonio. What I really wanted to do was adopt Jesús. I knew that would take months, which we didn't have. Plus, I knew his boss wouldn't cooperate because he wouldn't have such cheap labor at hand and that he didn't have to provide a place for him to live.

Just a few years later when Gerald and I returned to Spain for a visit, we asked about Antonio and Jesús. We were told that Jesús was in jail for stealing an apple from a fruit cart. I couldn't help but wonder, "Why? Why couldn't his story have turned out like Alicia's?"

❁

DURING OUR NINETEEN years in Madrid, Gerald and I also worked with children in the neighborhood where we lived. Much as I had done so many years ago in Mt. Zion church in Northern Kentucky, I tutored children at our dining room table. I remember one brother and sister well. One day when they came for their lessons, the girl – who was twelve – was crying uncontrollably. I hugged her and let her cry until she was ready to talk. Finally she said, "I said something mean to my father just because he couldn't get a glass of water for himself." I knew her father was so sick that he could no longer communicate verbally. That day I convinced her that her father loved her and that he understood she was frustrated about his illness. Not long afterward, the father died. Again, I comforted the children as they were now concerned about their mother who had spent so much time and energy caring for her husband while also working to make a living for her family.

As Gerald had done at Mt. Zion church in Kentucky so many years before, he also got involved in the lives of neighborhood children. One summer, a handsome young man came to VBS. After VBS was over, he continued to come to church. Gerald took him under his wing and taught him to use the projector to show films at church. One day the boy's mother came to see Gerald. She said, "That boy you like so much is on drugs. What are you going to do about it?" Gerald was shocked. After questioning the mother about how she knew about the drugs, Gerald told her he would find a place that could help her son.

When Gerald confronted the young man about the drugs, he tried to run away from him and climb the fence behind the seminary. Gerald chased and caught him.

Gerald made some telephone calls and found a place that could take the young man the following day. When he told the mother, she said her husband would let their son sleep in their house but she would not cook for him. So Gerald brought him to our house to eat. The next day Gerald took him to the appointed place. After Gerald left, the young man ran away and went home. At that, his mother called Gerald to ask once again what he planned to do about the situation.

Once again Gerald made some calls and found a facility with stricter security. There the young man received the help he needed and eventually was free to go home. Amazingly, his parents sent Gerald and me a beautiful vase – a gift that still means more to us that we can tell. And best of all, when we retired and left Spain, the young man was attending church.

❋

IT WAS ONCE AGAIN time for furlough – the last one that would be a full year. With each furlough, it was becoming harder and harder to be away from seminary responsibilities; yet, we knew this furlough would be special and that we wanted to stay in one location for the entire time since it would be Marsha's senior year of high school. We knew when we returned to Spain, we would return without her as she would stay in the States for college. During our furlough year, we wanted to help her learn how to manage a bank account, balance a checkbook, and take care of other details that would be new to her. She, like Linda, wouldn't be able to call home for advice or help, and letters were still taking several days to get to Spain and back.

At the end of that furlough year, Marsha graduated from Waggener High School in Louisville in 1973. Marsha chose to follow in her parents' and her sister's footprints and attend Georgetown College. When Gerald and I returned to Spain alone, it was difficult for all of us, but there were no easy remedies.

Thankfully, Marsha had her sister and new brother-in-law nearby. Linda and Rusty had married the year before, so Marsha was able to spend many weekends with them at their home in Louisville. She often brought her roommate, who was also a Missionary Kid, with her. Even though Joyce Reed had grown up in Israel, as MKs she and Marsha had many things in common. Plus, they both enjoyed Saturday morning pancake breakfasts at Linda's as well as talking about school problems or other issues with Marsha's big sister.

Marsha was an elementary education major, which proved perfect for her as over the years after graduation she has worked in an international setting with youth in camps and in counseling. She also earned a master in religious education degree from The Southern Baptist Seminary in Louisville. There she met her future husband, David Smith. Now, in 2015, they have lived in an international setting for more than thirty years and reared their two sons, Joel and Nathan, there. In recent years, Marsha also earned a second master's degree – this one in counseling, giving her skills she now uses daily.

That left Gerald and me with an empty nest, sorta. We still had many guests in our home.

❀

GERALD CONTINUED to keep a busy schedule. As usual, he added many extra responsibilities to his primary role as seminary president.

Gerald remained as president until 1978. Then he felt strongly that it was time for a national to become president, so he proposed to the board of trustees that he step down as president and that Jose Borrás take his place. The board enthusiastically agreed.

In actuality, Gerald and Sr. Borrás traded positions: President McNeely became Dean McNeely and Dean Borrás became President Borrás. Sr. Borrás was eminently qualified educationally and was highly respected among Spanish Baptists. He'd been elected four times to serve as president of the Spanish Baptist Union, the national organization of Baptists in Spain, and he was a beloved pastor. Gerald served as Dean until our retirement in 1989.

❀

THROUGH THE YEARS, even with Gerald's meticulous planning, sometimes some details had to be dealt with at the last minute. I was usually prepared with backup plans in case someone couldn't carry out a responsibility. And sometimes, even the back-up plan and the back-up planner needed help.

Once when Gerald was interim pastor of the English-language church in Madrid he needed me to be responsible for the Sunday night service at Alcobendas. That day as I was walking to church on the shoulder of the road, a car filled with young people swerved just as it reached me, causing me to fall. The driver continued on but did stop a little distance away to see what damage had been done. When the young people saw me get up, they continued on their way. They apparently didn't see that my knee was bleeding.

When I got to the church and the people saw my knee, they insisted on taking me to the hospital emergency room. I left a student in charge of the service, thinking the people could at least sing until I got back. At the emergency room, the doctor said I needed stitches and told me to get up on the table. He proceeded to light a cigarette. Being short, I struggled to get up onto the high table, but I finally managed. After he'd taken the first stitch, he took a draw on his cigarette, blowing smoke everywhere – including on me. He repeated that process four more times.

When we got back to church, the group was still singing and no one had prepared to preach. So they placed a chair for me to sit in and deliver the message. I refused the chair and delivered my message standing up. Those who'd been with me in the emergency room and had seen my wound told the others they knew the seminary church would grow because it had been sowed with Sra. June's blood! The knee healed, but the scar remained and still reminds me of that day.

I will be exalted among the nations,
I will be exalted in the earth.
Psalm 46:10b

FOURTEEN

❀

Kid Missionaries. That's what fellow-missionary Joe Mefford called our girls. And Linda and Marsha lived up to that moniker. Yes, they were Missionary Kids (MKs), the children of missionaries, but from a very early age they were developing a missions lifestyle of their own. They were Kid Missionaries.

Soon after we moved to Alicante two years into our first term of service, our four-year-old Marsha showed just how much sharing about Jesus was a part of her daily life. One day our next door neighbor who also had a four-year-old daughter came over to invite our girls to come to her apartment and play. On the arranged day she picked Linda and Marsha up and went to her apartment. I was happy for our girls to have a new playmate, and I felt safe with them in a nearby apartment.

They hadn't been gone long when our doorbell rang. When I opened the door, I saw the neighbor with our girls. Marsha was crying and Linda looked angry. The neighbor was gripping both girls by their shoulders as she demanded in Spanish, "Why didn't you tell me you go to that Baptist church in town? I don't want my daughter to play with a Protestant." She then threw Marsha across the front foyer where she hit the wall. The woman also tried to throw Linda but soon learned that throwing a stubborn, furious eight-year-old can be very hard. She then told my girls, "I don't want you to ever speak to my little girl. Even if you should see her on the street, I don't want you girls to ever have anything to do with my daughter." With that said, she stomped back to her apartment.

After she left I tried to explain to my girls that they should forgive our neighbor. I told them that she had acted as she did because she didn't know Jesus. We all agreed that we wouldn't play with or speak to the little girl again but that we would pray for her and her mother.

Some days later our neighbor came back to our apartment. This time she was much calmer. "What is your little girl teaching my child?" she asked. I told her I didn't even know that the children had seen each other, much less talked. She then said, "Yes, because you made a place for Marsha to play on your back balcony, I made one for my daughter, too. It's true that they haven't been playing together but they have been talking. Marsha has been teaching my daughter some sayings. Some of them are good, like *'Amáos los unos a los otros.'* (Translation: 'Love one another'.) I thought that was sweet. And *'Niños, obedeced a vuestros padres.'* (Translation: 'Children, obey your parents.') I like that, too."

The mother continued, "Today she taught something new. She said something I don't understand. Can you tell me what she was talking about? It was something like 'I don't have any silver or gold, but I'll give you what I do have. Get up and walk.' What does that mean?" By then I knew what had been happening – Marsha had been teaching her the Bible memory verses she'd been learning in Sunday school!

And so I said, "I know what it is. It's a story in the Bible." Then I told her the story of Peter and John as recorded in Acts chapter 3. In that passage, the two men healed someone who was sick and told him to get up and walk. After I'd finished, my neighbor said, "It's in what?"

"It's in the Bible," I replied.

"The Bible? What's a Bible?" she asked.

I told her to wait in our entrance hall or to come on into the living room while I went to get a Bible. I knew I had a box of New Testaments that a group of Woman's Missionary Union women had sent from the States. When I returned with the New Testament, I turned to Acts 3:6. Then she said, "My husband has a book like that. Wait a minute and I'll show you." She went quickly across the hall and returned with a small book – it wasn't a Bible; it was a dictionary. I explained that the books weren't the same, and I offered to give her the one I was holding. I told her there were many more good stories in the book. She was surprised that I wanted to give it to her and was hesitant about taking it. When I told her that some friends had given me the book and they wanted me to give it away, she was very happy and took the New Testament.

When I asked Marsha why she'd talked to the girl when her mother had specifically told her not to, Marsha said, "Well, you said she didn't know Jesus, so I was teaching her about Him." When I reminded her that she had been told not to speak to the girl, she replied, "Yes, but her mother said not to speak to her on the *street*. She didn't say anything about the balcony."

What could I tell her except that the girl's mother now had a Bible! And she had promised to read it!

A few days later as I was looking out my open window, my neighbor saw me from her window. She told me that she was still reading the New Testament that I had given her. In the following months, we had some good conversations in which she often asked me the meaning of what she had read.

Soon after that we moved back to Barcelona. Until the day we left, Marsha and her neighbor friend continued to play across their very high balcony playrooms, encouraged by her mother. Marsha continued teaching Bible verses to her friend. My Kid Missionary at work.

Our family continued to pray for that little girl and her mother after we moved to Barcelona. Our pastor in Alicante promised to follow up with them, too.

❁

LINDA, TOO, was a Kid Missionary. Over the years, the girls and I often went with Gerald to *El Hogar de Ancianos* (Home for the Aged) in Villafranca del Panades when Gerald preached there. (I will write more about that home in chapter sixteen.)

Linda, Marsha, and I would spend Sunday afternoon visiting with the *abuelos* (grandparents). Both the girls were very comfortable with the elderly residents and we soon found out just how comfortable the residents were with them: They argued about which resident the girls loved the most.

One day when Gerald wasn't available to preach, I was in charge of the evening service. I arrived early and sat near the front. When Linda and Marsha came a bit later, they found the building quite crowded. As they made their way down the aisle, they finally came to a pew near the front with only one person seated in it. That person happened to be one of the women who had been arguing about who the girls loved most. Of course, at the time neither the girls nor I knew about the argument, but I did think it was strange when the woman stood up and smirked at the other women as the girls entered her pew, as if to say, "See, I told you they loved me more."

Both Linda and Marsha loved the woman who ran the home with her husband. And Sra. Josefina Santacana returned that love. When we visited Villafranca, she would insist that we come to her home to eat or at least have refreshments. On one occasion, Sra. Santacana apologized because she hadn't had time to prepare anything special for us. She said, "I don't have anything in the house but canned peaches." While we were eating, our nine-year-old Linda said, *"Me encantan los melocotones en lata."* Translation: "I love canned peaches." After that, every time we visited, Sra. Santacana served canned peaches. That's what Kid Missionaries do – they consider the feelings of the other person before their own and they try to make the other person comfortable.

When we had a meal with Sra. Santacana, she didn't have enough dishes to be able to serve each course for her family of four and our family of four at the same time, so she washed dishes between the three courses. Not only did that delay the meal, but it was also exhausting for her. As much as I wanted to help her or even suggest that we use the same plate for the *segundo plato* (second course), I knew that I couldn't. I knew Sra. Santacana would have been mortified. Unlike Americans – who dine more casually than Spaniards and are generally assumed to be welcome in each other's kitchens – Spaniards are more formal. Though Sra. Santacana and I were close friends, my family and I were considered honored guests when we visited in the Santacana home. She was to serve us.

But none of those customs stopped our Linda. One day she could no longer stand to see Sra. Santacana working so hard by herself, so she went to the kitchen and offered her help. At first Sra. Santacana refused, but because she was so fond of Linda she finally handed her a dish towel. In fact, that made Linda like a daughter to her. From then on, Linda always helped her in the kitchen, and no one ever said a word about it. Kid Missionary at work.

The girls often asked Gerald and me why Sra. Santacana always wore black. We told them that after her mother had died she had worn black as a sign of mourning – as was the custom in Spain. By the time we met her, her husband's mother also had died, so once again she was in mourning and wearing black. Because she had worn black for so long, she had simply gotten used to it and had never worn anything colorful after that.

I guess Linda must have spent a lot of time thinking about that, because some time later when we were visiting Sra. Santacana, Linda said to her, "You have such a pretty face, I would love to see you in something blue." Sra. Santacana didn't say a word. The next time we saw her she was wearing a blue dress and she did look lovely. Once again, our Kid Missionary at work.

Your attitude should be the same as that of Christ.
Philippians 2:5

FIFTEEN

❀

From my first Sunday in Spain when I was faced with a personal choice about head coverings for women and felt the need to find a way to bridge the gap between Scripture and a tradition that to me was a symbol of submission, I was constantly concerned about the status of women both in society and in our churches.

In the 1950s when Gerald and I first went to Spain, many Spanish people thought a female's brain wasn't capable of developing like a male's brain. (Remember, that had once been the thinking of many Americans, too.) That thinking even affected the lives of young girls, which I encountered when the daughter of one of our seminary students suddenly dropped out of elementary school. When I talked with her mother, she said that her daughter – who'd been Marsha's playmate – had liked school so much she often dreamed about it. When she and her husband had told their doctor, he'd advised them to take her out of school because school was obviously affecting her brain. "Female brains are not strong enough to be forced to learn," he'd told them. (Fortunately, over the years those ideas about women have changed.)

In those early years, however, that thinking also influenced most of the wives of the students in the seminary, even though many were very bright. They simply believed such thinking to be true. For example, one young woman in one of my Old Testament classes lived with the residual of such thinking even after her husband had taught her to read after they married. When it came time for an exam, she was scared that she wouldn't pass. I helped her as much as I could. She persevered and she passed!

Another woman in one of my classes told me she could only read a little and that only slowly. She also told me that she'd never read a book. I felt she could read more if she were challenged and looked for a way to help her. The seminary library often received children's books in Spanish that we hadn't ordered, so I asked her to do me the favor of reading a new children's book to see if I should keep it or send it back. Sometime later she rushed into the library and swung me around and around – though she was smaller than I – saying, *"Lo hice. lo hice. leí un libro."* Translation: "I did it, I did it. I read a book!" As a teacher, I couldn't think of a better reward than that.

❁

THE LACK OF freedom for women affected ministry in other ways as well. For example, a Spanish woman couldn't travel by train, bus, or air without her husband's written permission. One day at an executive board meeting in Barcelona of the Spanish Woman's Missionary Union, I saw just how much that could impact a woman's daily life.

That day one of the board members told us she'd almost been late to catch the train from another city in Spain in coming to the meeting. It seemed that when it came time to board, she'd realized she'd forgotten to get a note from her husband giving her permission to travel to Barcelona. Fortunately, in the boarding confusion no one had asked for her *permiso* and she'd been able to get to the meeting.

When she told us what had happened we all worried about her return trip home, so she said she would call her husband and ask him what to do. He said he would inform the station personnel that she had his permission to return home, and all would be well. However, some of the women in our group continued to be fearful for her until she called to tell us she was safely home. Those women knew in a way I never could just how serious the situation could have been.

❁

DURING THE EARLY history of the seminary, the female presence on campus was that of wives supporting their student-husbands. While some training for the role of pastor's wife was offered, it was unstructured and dependent on which missionary wives were available to teach and what their expertise was. In the mid-1970s, however, after the seminary moved to Madrid, the study program for the wives became more structured. (I wrote about this in chapter thirteen.) Plus, in the mid-1970s, single women began enrolling at the seminary, preparing to fulfill their calling.

The possibilities for women were becoming endless. That a single woman could train to fulfill her own call was a precious reminder to me of how I had followed my call by saying "Yes" to wherever God was going to lead me. When Gerald and I had said "Yes" to God, we'd known so little of what He was actually calling us to do. What we did know was that all He asked of us was obedience. As women began attending the seminary, we prayed that many more would continue to hear God's call and be obedient. We prayed that they, too, would follow God step by step.

❀

THROUGHOUT MY years in Spain, ministering through Woman's Missionary Union (WMU) was one of the ways I was able to join fellow missionaries in helping women see their worth in the eyes of God. The organization – which is based in Birmingham, Alabama – has made a difference in the lives of women around the world from the time it began in 1888. Through WMU, women have been empowered to fulfill God's commandment to share the love of Christ with all the peoples in the world. Through WMU, women have been imbued with God-given perseverance and passion to encourage other women to see their own worth as well. And that was true in Spain. To encourage Spanish women to be all God meant for them to be was one of my greatest joys.

Looking back, in my mind's eye I see many women in Spain who led the way in showing the value in God's kingdom of all women – regardless of their economic status or educational background. They were both Spanish women and American missionaries. Among many, many others were Noemi Bonet, Indy Whitten, Josefina Santacana, Betty Law, Noemi Tejerina, Lila Mefford, and Pepita Pastor.

In my early years in Spain, the strength of WMU ebbed and flowed depending on government restrictions, travel issues, and the expectations of the role of the organization and the role of women. Even in the most difficult times for Spanish Baptists, however, publication of WMU materials was a major asset to their work, especially because of the printing services provided by the Salvadó family in Barcelona. The national WMU magazine – *Nuestra Labor* (Our Task) – faithfully charted the progress of women's groups in local churches and published original and compelling programming material for women's meetings as well as resources for children's and youth missions organizations. Ironically, one day when the police raided the Salvadó print shop, confiscated and then banned much of our Spanish Baptist literature, they left *Nuestra Labor* alone because it was for women! How threatening could it be if it were for women! To this day, *Nuestra Labor* continues to be a strong and encouraging link between women in the churches throughout Spain.

Through printed materials such as *Nuestra Labor,* Spanish women learned they had an essential role to play in spreading the love of Christ throughout their country; the task wasn't just for men. They learned that according to Scripture, women are not limited to supporting roles. Women can lead. Women can organize themselves and learn how to teach others.

Therefore go and make disciples of all nations.
Matthew 28:19a

SIXTEEN

❀

On Nov. 20, 1975, Generalíssimo Francisco Franco died after thirty-six years as dictator. Two days later, his protégé and heir to the throne, Juan Carlos, was crowned king. We all waited with fear and trepidation to see what he would do. Would he be a puppet of Franco and continue his reign of oppression? Could he see that certain freedoms would make Spain more appealing to the rest of Europe? Would new freedoms open doors to economic progress?

In the days immediately following Franco's death, tensions were high in Madrid and throughout the country. Linda and her husband, Rusty, were visiting us at the time and vividly remember Franco lying in state and hearing much speculation about what was going to happen next.

We all breathed a sigh of relief when Juan Carlos introduced a constitutional monarchy that would lift many bans and restrictions. That was a giant step even though many prejudices and misinformation regarding Baptists remained in the minds of the public. While a 1967 "Law of Religious Liberty" had eased some governmental restrictions, churches still had been required to register with the government. Now under Juan Carlos, things changed. In 1978, a new Constitution confirmed the right of all Spanish citizens to religious freedom and began the process of disestablishing Catholicism as the state religion. Juan Carlos orchestrated a widely praised transition to democracy that became a model for other countries making a similar transition.

At last, churches and seminaries could post identifying signs. At last, Baptists could tell their children details about the years when they hadn't been able to openly carry their Bibles and when they had to keep windows closed or whisper songs during worship services to avoid being heard by the *Guardia Civil*, Franco's personal army. At last, they could talk openly about how churches were closed by governmental authorities and locks and seals put on the doors. (In our early years in Spain, fifteen Baptist churches had been closed by the government.) And even though strong prejudices still remained, at last Baptists and other evangelicals no longer had to live with facing daily governmental restrictions; such issues had become a part of history.

Now, we Baptists could gather in large numbers to celebrate our faith. Soon attendance at conventions of the *Union Evangelica Baptist Española* (UEBE) grew so large that none of our churches was large enough to host the meetings. From then on, the UEBE had to rent a large municipal building and make sure the host city had adequate hotels to accommodate everyone who attended the meetings. Sometimes even the mayor or another dignitary from the host city would come to our meetings. We stood in awe. Only a few years before, it would have been impossible to imagine such a thing. Clearly, the Spanish people were beginning to know Baptists and were beginning to become aware that we posed no threat.

❖

THE ERA OF freedom had indeed begun, but we never wanted to forget what our Spanish brothers and sisters had experienced during Franco's thirty-six-year reign of terror. We wanted always to remember how they'd overcome. Churches, pastors, laypeople, and missionaries across the country had felt the strong arm of Franco's regime. And yet Spanish Baptists had remained strong and God had been faithful. Space doesn't permit me to write as many stories as I'd like, so I will recount but a few as representative of the many.

In one case, the chief of police of the town had come to a church to stop services. A church member had met him outside the building and had begun witnessing to him even as he'd answered the policeman's questions and as the service had continued inside. Then the policeman had begun to cry and had said, "I was sent here to stop this meeting. Please ignore that I'm here." And he'd gone inside the church and listened to the rest of the service.

Many pastors had been threatened and fined. Some had been placed under house arrest, while others had been put in jail. Pastor Jose Nuñez, whose church in Madrid was closed with a government seal, had twice stood trial and had been under house arrest for eighteen months. Finally, in 1963 his church had been reopened.

Sr. Benjamin Santacana, the pastor of the Villafranca church, had been sentenced to jail for preaching, the church had been closed, and members of the congregation had been fined. (Several years later – to our joy – Gerald and I attended the baptism of the daughter of the judge who'd sentenced Sr. Santacana to jail.)

Since most of the pastors had been bi-vocational, it had been easy for the authorities to harass them. When the authorities would learn the men were leading churches for *Protestantes,* they'd often see that they lost their secular jobs.

Church members, too, had been threatened, and their response often had been beyond words. To this day I cannot erase one experience from my mind. As I was heading toward the Metro (subway) from our apartment in Barcelona, I saw Pastor Sr. Samuel Rodrigo from Bona Nova Baptist Church exiting the subway. When I caught up to him, I could tell he was visibly shaken. He told me he'd just come from the Salvadó print shop that printed our Baptist materials and Bibles and that the printer had told him that government agents had threatened to shut the shop down as well as lock up all the Bibles he'd printed. The agents had finally agreed to lock all the Bibles in one room but had taken the key to that room with them. They'd told the printer not to try to open the door to the room and not to print any Baptist magazines and other evangelistic materials.

True to their nature, that hadn't stopped Spanish Baptists. They simply had changed the names of their magazines. *El Eco de la Verdad* (The Echo of Truth) became *El Eco.* The woman's magazine *Nuestra Labor* (Our Task) remained the same – to the government, it was just a woman's magazine and hadn't been considered important enough to be included in the printing ban. They hadn't realized it contained material for children and youth, too. Once when Pastor Rodrigo had been arrested and taken to the court house, he'd been asked if he wanted something to read while he waited. He'd been handed a copy of *Nuestra Labor*. What irony! The authorities must have thought the magazine carried no threat.

In another case, Gerald and fellow-missionary Joe Mefford had just finished leading a service in a village when they saw government officials standing outside the building, writing down the names of all the villagers who were present in the service. Then the officials had fined all of them. But that wasn't the end of the story. Later, when Gerald had been preaching to a group of American sailors who were in port in Barcelona, he had told about the incident. The sailors had been so touched that they had voluntarily taken up an offering to pay the fines of those believers.

During those years, it hadn't been unusual for children and teens to be expelled from public school when it was discovered that their parents attended a *Protestante* or a Baptist church – the authorities didn't know the difference.

Sometimes persecution had come from family members. Linda remembers a blind girl who attended a missions camp we put on. She'd become a believer there. When she told her family, they threw her out of the house and drove her out of town. No one knew what became of her.

Elderly evangelical believers also had suffered. When they would move to state-run homes for seniors, they often were treated as second-class citizens just because they were evangelicals. In some of the government-run homes for the elderly, food and even water had been withheld until those dear believers had begged or repented.

Again in spite of the difficulties, Spanish Baptists had wanted to provide a place where elderly believers could live in peace, and God had provided. After the parents of Sr. Santacana – about whom I wrote above – had died and left him some money, he and his wife had knelt by their bed and asked God to show them how He wanted them to use their inheritance.

Not long after, Sr. and Sra. Santacana had heard about another case of persecution of a Baptist living in a state home. Immediately, they'd known they had the answer to their prayer. They then had found a house in Villafranca for *El Hogar de Ancianos* and had become the first two staff members, cooking, cleaning, and caring for elderly Baptists, most of whom were women.

American missionaries had to be on guard, as well. In our thirty-two years in Spain, Gerald was arrested only one time. That day he had been distributing evangelistic literature and witnessing about Jesus in the city of Huesca. Because he was an American citizen, he hadn't been detained. He, however, had been strongly admonished never to return to Huesca. He never did. We were always aware of our non-citizen status and the tenuousness of the political climate in Spain. When we were living in Barcelona, we even made contingency plans should things become dangerous for our family: Gerald would stay at the seminary, and I would take the girls by train to Figueras near the Spanish-French border. There, the girls and I would take another train into France. If we'd succeeded in our escape, we then would only be a few minutes away from Perpignan, France. Of course, we didn't tell Linda and Marsha about these plans; in fact, they only learned about them when they were well into adulthood.

As I've already written, as time had passed the governmental restrictions had become fewer. Still, it wasn't until after Franco's death that we saw major changes.

❊

FAST FORWARD TO 1989, thirty-two years after Gerald and I had first set foot on Spanish soil. We could hardly believe that it would be time for us to retire after one last furlough. After more than three decades of constant, intense ministry, Gerald was exhausted. We knew it was time to move back to Louisville and spend time with our family. We looked forward to living near Linda and Rusty and our grandchildren, Lisa and Matt. We looked forward to seeing first-hand how Rusty and Linda were helping to promote missions in their church. And we looked forward to seeing Marsha and David and our grandchildren, Joel and Nate, who were spending more leave time in the States. (As is traditional, we would spend our first year back in the States as a "furlough year" on deputation for the Foreign Mission Board; that is, we would be traveling and speaking on behalf of the Board. Thus, we officially retired in 1990, after thirty-three years with the Board.)

There were many moving good-byes at the seminary and there were many memorable moments with people in the many churches that we'd helped. Churches graced us with plaques and flowers. There were touching farewells in homes of Spanish friends and in churches. One special moment came as we sat around the Meffords' kitchen table in Denia, reliving the past and remembering all the funny moments we'd experienced together. And at the meeting of all the Southern Baptist missionaries serving in Spain at that time, we were treated to fellow-missionaries' memories of us.

And there were those practical considerations. We had to decide what possessions to take to the States and what to leave behind. A wonderful moment came when we gave our precious piano to the Herrara family (the family with the many children in the Alcobendas Church about whom I wrote in chapter thirteen). The generosity of Jane Points at Mt. Zion Church who had made that piano possible for us would live on.

Then it was time to go. We squeezed in one more trip to represent Spain at a meeting of European Baptist Federation before we left for the States. This time, the meeting was held in Budapest, Hungary. We couldn't help but remember our first EBF meeting thirty years before in 1959 in Berlin, before the Berlin Wall was put up. The world had changed and we had changed, but the power of the gospel remained the same.

The Bible passage most often quoted by evangelicals in Spain during our years there was Romans 8:35, 37-39: "Who will separate us from the love of Christ? Shall trouble or hardship or persecution or famine or nakedness or danger or sword? No, in all these things we are more than conquerors through Him who loved us. For I am convinced that neither death nor life, neither angels or demons, neither the present nor the future, nor any powers, neither height nor depth, nor anything else in all creation will be able to separate us from the love of God that is in Christ Jesus our Lord." (NIV)

How faithfully our dear Spanish brothers and sisters had lived out that verse. Their constancy and faithfulness would be a model for generations to come. And they will live in our hearts forever. *Alabado sea Dios.* Praise be to God.

APPENDIX 1
Names And Honorifics

✿

I n Spain, even after a woman is married, she uses her family name followed by the word *de* (of) and her husband's family name. Here is an example: My given name is June and my maiden name is Hall. My husband's family name is McNeely. So I am June Hall de McNeely. The American way of dealing with women's names makes no sense to the Spanish.

Another custom is the use of the words *Don* and *Doña*. *Don* is placed before a male's given name and *Doña* is placed before a female's given name. Since both are titles of courtesy or of special recognition, they aren't used for everyone. The recognition may be for higher education or something else that sets that person apart. For example, the title can be used if a person's son or daughter has earned a degree, and thus has set their parents apart from their peers.

Using the honorifics Don or Doña requires using the first name. When I was addressed as Doña June, some Americans thought that was too personal but it was actually the Spanish way of honoring me.

I had an additional problem with my name, Beverly June. The Spanish word for June is *Hunie,* which sounds strange and is hard to pronounce. So I decided to try using Beverly instead. When I told a Spanish friend, she said, "Oh yes, Señora Veberly." I'd forgotten that in some areas of Spain "b's" and "v's" are the same sound. I decided to stay with June.

And then there are the titles Señor, Señora, and Señorita. For example, while Sr. Fontanet's first name is Felix, no missionary would ever address him as Felix. We always used the formal *Señor,* or in certain circumstances, *Don Felix.* Nationals did the same with us missionaries. It was a matter of courtesy and respect.

APPENDIX 2
June's Recipe for Brownies

❁

Brownies

7 Tbsp cocoa
½ cup butter, melted
2 eggs
1 cup sugar
1 cup flour
¾ tsp salt
1 t. vanilla
1 cup chopped nuts

Beat eggs. Add sugar, then flour
and cocoa very slowly.
when well blended, add melted butter
and nuts. Add vanilla.
  Spread over bottom of
buttered pan and bake in hot oven
20 minutes.
  Mark off in squares or strips
as soon as removed from oven.

Handwritten by June at age 90

March 2015

APPENDIX 3
A Brief Account of the Acquisition of the Property in Denia

Sr. Vicente and Sra. Josefa Pastor were led to faith in Christ in 1914 by a Swedish Baptist missionary who had come to Denia looking for raisins to export. As the first Baptists in Denia, their baptisms presented a challenge. The first attempt at 9 a.m. on a beach failed when word got out that Protestants were baptizing there and the police and a group of local citizens showed up wielding sticks. The next morning, they met at 4 a.m. – under cover of darkness and in secret – and were baptized.

When news of their baptisms got out, Sr. Pastor lost his job at a local toy factory. Both their families disowned them, causing them to become homeless. In order to survive, they raised enough food to eat on a piece of property owned by Sr. Pastor's father. Located on a hillside, it was studded with almond trees.

Soon after their baptism, the couple began praying every day for hours at a time on that property. For seven years, they kept praying. Then one day they felt God speak very clearly to their hearts. God said, *"Esta tierra es para mi."* Translation: "This property is for Me."

Later when Sr. Pastor's father sold the property, the couple put that word from God out of their minds, thinking "How could God's promise be true?" To make a living, Sr. Pastor opened his own toy shop and also began making guitars. The couple also began a church in their home. Their son, Joaquin, was the pastor of that church for seventeen years.

It was Joaquin who first had the vision for a school and retreat center on the property that his grandfather had owned. Then in 1961, the family learned that the Southern Baptist Foreign Mission Board had purchased seven acres for a Baptist camp in Denia. Sr. Vicente and Sra. Josefa were on hand for the announcement and when they heard it, they began to cry – it was the land about which God had told them *"Esta tierra es para mi."* All through the years, the couple had told no one about God's promise to them. Sr. Vicente told those gathered that day, *"Hoy la promesa de Dios ha sido cumplida."* Translation: "Today, God's promise has been fulfilled."

For many years that site served Spanish Baptists as a retreat center. And even later, a day care center and a well-respected elementary school opened on the site. In 2015, the land is owned by the Baptist Evangelical Union – the national body of Spanish Baptists – and the day care and school are operated by the church that Sr. Vicente and Sra. Josefa started. Today, Jorge Pastor, the grandson of the elder Pastors, is the pastor. Gerald and I are proud to have had him as a student at *Seminario Teológico Bautista*.

ACKNOWLEDGMENTS

I am deeply grateful to my family who patiently helped me during my recovery after my two strokes. Gerald, Edna, Mary Catherine, Keith, Ida, our children, and our grandchildren all helped in my recovery. Some spent the night with me, others visited with me daily and tirelessly helped the aides care for me. Mother would be so proud of us all!

I thank my daughters for helping me with this manuscript. However, any errors in memory are purely my own.

Linda reviewed my old letters and transcribed my stories for this book even when they were barely legible. Marsha was a wonderful proofreader, even from overseas!

Gerald was my constant source of encouragement. He even took over my daily household activities in order to free me to write.

I am grateful for the honor of working with Joyce Martin on this project. Joyce is a professional who handled my story with great care and respect. I value her friendship and her wisdom.

I thank the members of Women on Mission groups, Girls in Action groups, and other organizations of Woman's Missionary Union who never forget to pray for missionaries whom they may never have the chance to meet. Let me assure you that we missionaries feel every one of those prayers. Don't ever stop lifting us up!

ABOUT THE AUTHORS

JUNE HALL MCNEELY and her husband, Gerald, served as Southern Baptist missionaries in Spain for thirty-three years. A native Kentuckian, June is a graduate of Georgetown College in Georgetown, Kentucky, and holds a master in library science degree from Spalding College in Louisville, Kentucky. She did further study at the University of Barcelona (Spain).

June and Gerald have two adult children – Linda and Marsha; four grandchildren – Lisa, Matt, Joel, and Nate; and several great-grandchildren. They are blessed with son-in-laws Rusty and David.

Since their retirement in 1990, June and Gerald have made their home in Louisville.

JOYCE SWEENEY MARTIN is an author, editor, and writing coach in Louisville, Kentucky. A native Kentuckian, she is a graduate of Georgetown College in Georgetown, Kentucky, and The Southern Baptist Theological Seminary in Louisville. She and her minister-husband, Larry, served for nineteen years as missionaries with the Southern Baptist Home Mission Board (now the North American Baptist Board) in Detroit, Michigan; Boston, Massachusetts; and at the board's home office in Atlanta, Georgia. She has written hundreds of articles for regional and national religious newspapers and magazines. She also has been a newspaper editor, and is the author or co-author of nine books. (June Hall McNeely's father and Larry Martin's grandmother were siblings.)

CPSIA information can be obtained at www.ICGtesting.com
Printed in the USA
LVOW07s1339020615

440740LV00004B/5/P